Belle Journal

A Literary Journal for the Modern Southern Belle

Volume I

As Southerners, we are tied to a land that is soaked in history and in emotion. The South is a living paradox, being deceivingly simple while consistently complex. Its contradictions generate reasons to ache and to rejoice…to dance and to grieve. Living in a land where injustice rests within beauty, the "Southern Experience" is brimming with stories of humor and of sorrow. At the center of all this chaos, there is always a Southern woman who either stands strong or crumples to the floor.

A "Southern Belle" is a commonly misunderstood phenomenon. We are not the fragile debutantes who evolved into stereotypes. We are resilient and wise beyond our years. We are the eyes and the hearts of the South and the keepers of its haunting memories.

"Belle" is simply a name for the soul that exists in every Southern woman. To be a Belle means to run towards life with a smile and an ear that delights in the stories it hears. A Southern Belle laughs with strangers and sings by herself, and you will find her at every turn and in every moment of the Southern Experience.

Belle Journal is a compilation of literary and visual work by Southern Belles. It is also a tribute to the magical Belles of the past and the present. Thank you to every Belle who submitted a piece of your heart to this journal.

Belle Journal would not exist without the time and energy of Robin Rentrope, Sarah Bailly, Ellen Ogden, Georgia Frederick, Logan Kinamore, Amanda Harb, Emily Thibodeaux, Chelsea Rainwater and Tom Harang.

A special shower of praise is due to Amelia Tritico for her unending dedication to formatting and editing our beautiful finished product.

Thank you for reading and thank you for sharing.
May you be well and, above all, be southern.

Janey Hogan
Belle/Editor/Tom Sawyer

Table of Contents

Poetry

Prose

Artwork

Masthead

Editor
Janey Hogan

Designer/Associate Editor
Amelia Tritico

Poetry Editor
Sarah Bailly

Editorial Assistant
Amanda Harb

Art Editors
Ellen Ogden
Georgia Frederick

Magnolia Artwork
Ellen Ogden

Cover Image
Mercedes Jelinek

Selection Committee

Emily Thibodeaux	Ellen Odgen
Georgia Frederick	Tom Harang
Logan Kinamore	Sarah Bailly

Amanda Harb

Logo Design/Web Editor
Robin Rentrope

This first volume of Belle Journal was funded by financial contributions from lovely human beings. We wish to thank the following major benefactors for their generous donations:

T.J. Dellinger, Daena Lower, Sam Tritico, Shante Williams, Aurelia Davila Pratt, Michael "Girth" Patterson, Emily DeLorge, Jessica Pierce, Anne Harb, Kathryn Wart, Patricia Mire Watson, Lori Corrigan, Jennifer Ator, Wendy Monistere, Cindy Pechon, Teresa King, Ellen Ogden, Nicole Stillwell, Elizabeth Edwards, Lynn Cornelison, Ashley Hemm, Rachel Hogan, Daniel LeBlanc, Vincent Paviglianiti, Jordan Causey, Jill Ogden, Stephanie Kadel Taras, Frank and Melinda Tritico, Jonathan Moser, Sang Ho, Josephine Ennis, Tom and Lila Hogan, Ruby Johnson, Edward J. DeLorge, Brian Habisreitinger, Whitney Turner, Stephen Frederick, Julie Barrett

For a full list of all financial contributors to Belle Journal, please visit www.bellejournal.com.

Southern Woman

I never go to a person's house
that I don't remove the walls,
rearrange the furniture,
take out the lockers,
and transplant the trees.
There is one exception – my own.

~ Gladys Cagle Tritico Stoker

Georgia Frederick

Jacques de Grille

Lori Wainwright

Way down south on the bayou in a boat,
Sailed little Jacques de Grille and his pet bullfrog Croak.

Now Jacques de Grille had an idea - it went like this right here,
He thought with Croak a-croaking loud, he'd draw other bullfrogs near.

He'd catch them in this net he had and get them in the boat,
And then he'd put them in the two big pockets on his coat.

And when he had enough of them, he'd take them home and then,
He'd put them in the cage with Croak, so Croak could have some friends.

Now Jacques de Grille he never thought he'd catch this many frogs!
Why before he left his pockets bulged like the sack of Santa Clause.

So away down the bayou sailed Jacques de Grille in his boat,
Not only with his pet bullfrog, but with all these friends for Croak.

And yes, he took them home with him - seventeen in all.
He was just making it around the corner when he heard Mama de Grille a-call.

"Jacques de Grille, the supper's ready. Leave those muddy boots outside.
But don't you leave that coat out there or I'll skin you alive."

Now Jacques de Grille he knows better than to back talk Mama at all,
So those boots stayed on the porch and that coat got hung in the hall.

Right about in the middle of supper, what do you suppose little Jacques hears,
But one of those bullfrogs and he sounded so near!

So Jacques, he chewed his food fast and was just about to swollar
When that ole bullfrog jumped on his sister's head and boy did she hollar!

Jacques, he moved fast, and he caught that frog against the wall,
Then what do you supposed he spied, but sixteen more a-coming down the hall.

After that it was frog mania - bullfrogs everywhere!
And poor little Jacques knew he was in trouble when he heard his mama swear.

"Jacques de Grille, you catch these bullfrogs and don't you miss a-one.
I want them all back in the bayou before the rising sun."

So Jacques, he moved like lightning and he caught them everyone.
And when he had that last one, to the bayou he did run.

He ran like it was daytime, 'round the corner and 'cross the woods.
If he hadn't been there when he did it, he wouldn't have thought he could.

He emptied out his pockets and those frogs all hopped away.
But now he knew that he could catch them if he liked, another day.

"I'll come back here tomorrow," thought Jacques. "I'll bring my boat.
But next time I guess I'll settle, for fewer friends for Croak."

"Decatur St. Double Exposure"

Carly Melancon

"Silhouette"

Amanda Harb

it's hard to believe in summer love when the only air conditioning you have is one window unit and that's busted

Anne Delatte

i think a lot about when i was a kid with the bayou in my backyard and there were a lot of
mosquitoes
and then to balance it out i think some about driveways and taxes and traffic lights
but there are still a lot of mosquitoes

then i tell you i wish we could send this place in and exchange it for something good
but i'm pretty sure the original packaging's damaged
i guess we could always say we found it this way
you say there are some good things about it
and at the same time we both say 'like me'

we are quiet for a while and pretend
to drink our coffee

you say don't be so down on the town you grew up in
i say it'd be rude to compliment a shithole, mama didn't raise no liars, etcetera
you say why don't you leave then
i say why don't you

so you leave

and by leave i mean you go into the bathroom and slam the door
because goddammit you pay half the rent too

then i think about locking the back door
but it is too hot for home invasions and anyway
those mosquitoes are stealthy bastards
they will find a way in

"Heidi"

Molly Gardner

God Bless Bonbons

Emily Bufford

It wasn't my fault his momma was crazy. She didn't even believe diabetes was real until they had to cut her leg clean off. We threatened her and told her time and again that all the sugar in those bonbons was going to kill her. She never responded very well to threats. A card lady friend of hers told me about one time when she was playing bridge at a friend's house years and years ago. Another lady threatened her life because Momma was cheating. They started hollering and screaming across that lace tablecloth, and wouldn't you know that lady—some say she was likely three hundred pounds of lady—laid there on top of Momma, beating on her like Jesus was never going to come. Momma never shut her mouth off. She kept screaming and cussing at that lady punching on her until blood came out her nose and she was missing at least one tooth.

And today his old Momma's been living in our trailer for one year, seven months, and twenty days. And I have been suffering her craziness all that time, but by tonight I won't be anymore.

Steve and I met just after high school was done. We'd gone to different schools, so we weren't sweethearts or anything like that. My best marks were in English class, but Steve's were in shop class. My family—really only me and my daddy—had just moved closer in to town after my graduation. We had lived far out; so far I had to walk five miles just to get to the school bus stop. Then we moved into an apartment building. It had been an extended-stay motel, but the new owners cleaned it out, fixed it up, and turned it into apartments. It was so strange for me to be so close to town and to people. For the first time I got to watch cable TV downstairs in the laundry room whenever I wanted.

One afternoon, bored as a pumpkin in a patch, I was at home

mopping the floors in my clogs. I opened the apartment door so the floors could dry up right quick as I made my way from stove to fridge. I was singing and dancing while I mopped. But then I accidentally bootscootinboogied my foot into the mop pail. My other foot went up, my head went down, and my shoe flew off. Next thing I knew, I heard a yell and moan from outside the apartment door. I picked up my soggy, soapy self and went to see what had happened. Splayed out on the floor was a young man bleeding from the nose, looking very confused, and holding my clog.

"This yours?" he asked, holding up my shoe.

"Yessir. I'm so sorry about that. I was mopping and somehow my foot got stuck in the bucket and down I went."

"Are you hurt? Let me help you sit down." He got up quick and pulled a plastic lawn chair over for me. "My name's Steve." He held my hand all gentleman-like as I sat.

"Hi Steve. My name's Lara." I used the washing rag from my back pocket to wipe the blood from under his nose.

About a year after that my daddy died, but before he did Steve was able to ask him for my hand in marriage. A year after that Steve and I were getting married. All it took was one bloody nose for us to fall in love.

Steve and my ceremony was just beautiful. We had it down by the dock, which is what Steve wanted, of course. I only agreed to have it at the dock if we could have the ceremony at sunset. Steve asked what for, and I told him it was because of all the pretty colors. He just ran his hand through his hair, smiled with his square teeth, and kissed me on the forehead. So we had it all down by the docks at sunset on a Wednesday. I picked Wednesday because the word kind of sounds like weddings-day. Everything we needed to rent was also a lot cheaper on Wednesdays. His momma wore a white pants suit, but I didn't say nothing at all. No one was going to ruin my day. It was hellish convincing the silk-flower company to let me rent them for use down by the docks. Eventually the company said I could use only the polyester flowers and not the actual silk ones. I said that was just fine by me and that we'd even spray some de-stink solution on them after we were all done.

My color of choice was peach, but not everything could match. Steve had his daddy's tuxedo to wear, which was a pinch small but no one seemed to notice, but we didn't have a matching cummerbund. So we had Aunt Dorris sew some cummerbunds together for us. Only, Aunt Dorris can't remember things real good, so when we said peach to her on the phone, she had forgotten by the time she went to the fabric store. She bought all pale yellow satin. It was half-price, so Steve was happy. So when we stood together at the altar Steve and all his groomsmen were wearing their pale yellow things and me and all my maids were wearing our peach things. The silk flower company didn't have a bouquet of polyester flowers in peach because the last woman who had used it puked at the altar, and they hadn't had it dry cleaned yet. So I had to use the lavender bouquet anyway. All of this turned out to be okay though, because Aunt Dorris forgot to bring the camera too. Some of Steve's buddies took pictures with their cell phones, and when I saw them I noticed that the peach dresses, pale yellow cummerbunds, and lavender flowers matched the colors of the sunset behind us. Like I said, our ceremony was just beautiful.

Since Steve and I couldn't afford a real honeymoon, Steve's boss offered that we could stay by his summer house for a few days; they were getting ready to sell it anyways. The house was about a two-hour drive from our trailer, and it was real nice. It was a big two-story house with five bedrooms and four and one-half baths. The hot water was always working; you never had to check and make sure the pilot light was on. It had a pool with the blue bottom so the water looked pretty, and it even had a waterfall. Only it would have been pretty, but the pumps were broken. The one thing Steve's boss asked was that we cleaned the pool up really nice for the real estate lady and that Steve fix the pump. So our first afternoon and night there Steve cleaned out the pool's inside and worked on the pump. Steve wouldn't let me lay a hand on a work tool—not a broom, skimmer, or wrench. He wanted this time to be special for me, and there isn't anything special about laboring on a pool. The next morning we took an au naturale swim in its beautiful blue water. These were the three happiest days of our marriage.

That's when Momma bulldozed into our lives. We were supposed to stay at Steve's boss' summer house for five days for our honeymoon, but we had to come back early. Momma had fallen at home—probably tripped over a stupid cat—and was in the hospital. Steve's one sister didn't live anywhere near us, and Steve's daddy had been dead for ages. This only left Steve to care for her, which really meant Steve and me. So we started sitting in the hospital with her whenever we could. I started working morning shift at the diner, even though the tips aren't as good.

Every single night while she was in the hospital, I cooked dinner for her and brought it on over. She, Steve, and I sat around her small-as-a-Chinese-take-out-box hospital room, with the TV shut off as Momma was used to, and ate dinner together. Every night when dinner was done, Steve left the room so Momma could have her sponge bath. She asked that I stay to keep her company, but I would of course be obliged to stare at the wall. Every night I asked her how she liked her dinner; every night she would say, "Well, there's always hope for tomorrow night." I kept my tongue locked in my mouth, but it burned as if Momma had poured serpent's poison on it. I just told myself that at some point she would leave the hospital and go home to her ten cats, which meant I would have to cook her dinner only once a month on the second Sunday. But that changed fast.

The doctors told us she didn't need an operation or anything, just some down time to get rest, so the doctor's released her pretty quick from the hospital. We brought her back to our trailer with us. I totally rearranged the entire house just for her. Steve and I didn't have much: one living room, one bedroom, one bathroom, one kitchen and one bed. So I dragged Steve and my double bed out into the living room by the TV with the end table squished between the foot of the bed and the Lazy Boy. I put our best one hundred-thread-count sheets on the bed, bought brand new pillows from Dollar General, and laid her favorite magazines on the end table. In Steve and my bedroom I fashioned a make-shift bed for us. It was all the extra comforters, bed spreads, and quilts that I could round up from the neighbors laid neatly on the floor in front of the couch. Then Momma came home.

At first I thought maybe Momma was just acting a little strange on account of being in the hospital, but later on I realized that she was just plain crazy.

"Oh dear, these windows just won't do. Darling, could you cover them with tinfoil so it won't be so bright in here. I like to nap in the afternoon." She tightened the strings holding on her oversized hat.

"Yes, Momma." And I set about taping tinfoil into the living room windows.

The next day, some time after Steve had been at work, Momma hollered loud while I was in the shower. I ran out the shower with soap in my eyes and barely wrapped in a towel. Momma had fallen down near the TV. "What is it Momma? What are you doing out of bed?" I kneeled by her side and checked her over to make sure nothing was broken.

"Oh, child, I just wanted to open up these windows; it's too dark in here." Her big watery, yellow eyes stared at me from under her blue painted lids.

"But, Momma, you asked me to cover them."

"Did I?"

"Yes, because you like to nap in the afternoons."

"Oh well, yes, sugar, but it's not the afternoon."

"Yes but—"

"No buts about it, sugar. It is not the afternoon."

Things went on like that, but I kept hope because she'd be leaving in four weeks just like the doctors said.

During her third week of staying with us I took Momma to the doctor for a follow-up visit. They said her blood work had come back from the lab when she was in the hospital after her fall, and it turned out she had diabetes. The doctors gave us a couple of pamphlets and made appointments for Momma to come see about her health and her new disease later on. That night, Steve and I had a talk.

"I want Momma to stay with us until she's all set up and understands what's going on with her sickness." Steve was always a straight-talker like that. He set his eyes on me.

"I really think she'd be more comfortable at home. I can take time off work to bring her to all her appointments and call her at lunch to make sure she's doing okay."

I really didn't think she'd be more comfortable at home, but I did think I'd be more comfortable in my home if she was gone. I just wanted Steve to think about it from all angles. I noticed Steve pick up one of the doctor pamphlets. He flipped open to the first page. I could see in his eyes he was struggling to get it. Diabetes is real confusing, like trying to get homemade bread to rise; too much heat and the whole thing collapses, not enough heat and the dough won't rise.

"I'll take care of those things, sweetheart." I pushed the papers down from his face and looked him in the eyes. I could see tears by the corners.

"She's the last parent we have between us, Lara. I'm not ready for her to die." He pressed his fingers against his eyes and hung his head.

He was scared to lose her, just like I was scared after my daddy's heart attack. I wasn't ready for my daddy to die either, but I couldn't do anything for him at all. I could try with Momma, for my Steve.

"Okay. I'll bring Momma over after bingo, and we'll have a chat with her about staying here. And I'll look at all these things to figure it out."

I gathered up the pamphlets, trying to keep them away from him because I knew—but would never say—that Steve could not read the big words and correct English inside them. "But those cats aren't allowed."

"We'll bring them to the pound." He grabbed my hand with his thick, rough fingers. "Thank you, Lara."

When Steve and I were sitting there I thought maybe I could help Momma regain her health and get her out in two months flat.

Six months later they took Momma's left leg. She played cards with other ladies from around the trailer park three times a week at night, and I knew it was those cackling old hens that were bringing Momma her bonbons. We told Momma she could not have her bonbons anymore. They were full of sugar and sure to kill her quick as a rattlesnake; Momma didn't listen. The morning after Momma was playing cards, I would wake up at four like usual and find Momma flipping channels on the TV like the devil was chasing her. I'd look at her face, and her eyes would be all twitchy, and at the corners of her wet, orange-lipsticked mouth would be bits of chocolate and vanilla bonbons. Steve never saw her like this because he picked up two shifts at the shipyard and a second job working the graveyard shift at the timber factory three times a week.

One night, after I had worked a double, I came on home to Momma. She had played cards with the ladies night before last, so at least I knew they wouldn't be there tonight. I put left-over pork chops with rice in the microwave for Momma and me to eat. This was one dish of mine that she never said anything about at all. She didn't say anything nasty; she didn't say anything nice. I figured it had to be one of her favorites, so as I was heating it up, I just knew that tonight was going to be a good night. I brought Momma her tray, switched off the TV as she liked, and we ate in silence. As I went to clear our plates in the sink, I swear I saw a smile crawl onto the left side of Momma's face. I was going to bed happy, until I went to lay myself down.

"Momma," I hollered from my bedroom. I could hear her bangle bracelets rattling in the front room. "Momma, where's my bed?"

She gave me a look of innocence from under her clumpy eyelashes. There wasn't anything left of my makeshift bed. The quilts, the comforters, the blankets—they were all gone, except Steve and my faded comforter with peaches on its off-white background.

"Momma?"

"Well, darling, all the neighbors came by today and needed their things back. So off they marched one by one. I suppose it's because of the lice." She looked down at her dry hands and cracked a few of her knuckles.

"What lice Momma?"

"Well, your lice, sugar dumpling."

"I don't have lice."

"Sure you do. Other night while you were cooking them pork chops I saw one stuck in your lovely chestnut hair. Steve reached right up and said 'Hey, you've got a bit of lice in your hair.' Then he plucked it out and tossed it to the sink."

"He said rice, Momma, not lice." I smiled at her, gentle as I could. "If Steve said it, how'd everybody find out?"

"One of my card ladies is a retired school nurse. I asked her if she knew how to get rid of lice. Maybe she told everybody else."

"Okay, Momma. Guess I'll just have to let everyone know tomorrow I don't have lice and may I please borrow their things again."

I went back to my bedroom and started laying down all Steve and my sweatshirts and jackets. I went to bed right then. No point in waiting. But as I tried to fall asleep, all I could hear was the rattling of Momma's bangles from the front room, like a rattler. That's how it was. If I wore pink lipstick, Momma would prefer me in red, but if I wore red lipstick she'd ask me if I weren't selling any extra services down by the diner. If I cooked eggs for breakfast, she'd prefer cereal, but if all I had time for was cereal, she'd want bacon. She watched those home-shopping channels for so long it actually burned the side bars into our TV. She also ordered from those places so frequently that I was going by the post office twice a week to return all the ridiculous things she bought. Premium steaks, triple fold ladders, juicing machines. I thanked God every day that those TV shopping places had such good return policies.

This was our three lives. Me dealing with Momma every moment at home and serving at the diner, and Steve at work all the time. Steve, bless his heart, tried to help with Momma, but he worked so much he wasn't ever home. He was working all those shifts to pay Momma's medical bills since she had to have her leg removed; she wasn't quite old enough for Medicare, and Medicaid kept giving us the run around about 'neglect of health.' I just couldn't tell Steve about her misbehaving. I'm all for honesty in a marriage, but Steve's a good boy and good boys love their mommas no matter what. I didn't want to stick him between a cactus and a briar patch. I just had to learn how to handle her, how to wear her down. I had time— God knows—trapped indoors with her every moment I wasn't working. I could have learned how to do it too, if things hadn't changed.

A year after they took her left leg, they had to take her right leg. After the second leg went, I didn't just have to assist her to the bathroom to take a shower, but I actually had to bathe her. The doctors gave us about a million different pamphlets to read and books to buy and rules to follow. Momma refused to read any of it, saying that nobody ever learned anything from a book they couldn't learn from trial and error. I looked at Momma's missing legs, and I knew that just was not true. The doctors said that Momma's pills, which she never took correctly, weren't going to cut it anymore. She had got to start checking her blood sugar regularly and taking insulin injections when she needed them. Fooling with the needles and the blood sugar machine wasn't a game; too much insulin in the needle could kill her, too little could kill her, avoiding veins wasimportant, not to mention air getting into a vein if we hit one. Steve and I agreed that I needed to take a break from the diner until we got all of this covered, until we both knew that Momma could do her own shots when she needed them.

It's been a month since I left work; she hasn't given herself a shot yet. I've been riding her like a trader man on a donkey to learn how to do it herself; she simply refuses. Steve comes home when he can, but most nights he gets stuck at work sleeping in a chair or the pickup until his next shift comes around. About a week ago he did get to come home, and Momma's forked liar's tongue came out.

"Oh, my Stevey boy! Come give your Momma a hug."

"Hey, Momma." He gave her a weak wave, but came and kissed me first. I saw her eyes light up with a golden fire, and the blacks went thin.

"You been taking good care of yourself like you're supposed to, right Momma?" I waited for her answer but already knew it.

"Of course honey pie, I'm just an old injecting fool over here. Kind of makes me feel like I'm addicted to the drugs, but I know better." She gave him a wink and a hug. Her bangles rattled.

"How many times you done it all by yourself, Momma?" he asked.

"Every day for the past ten days."

"Good then, looks like the diner might not have to suffer without you any more darlin'. Once Momma's leg's healed up you can go back to work."

I nodded yes to him. I let him think what he wanted. I only got to see him about ten hours in a week, so I didn't want to fill that precious time with worrying about Momma. He can't help anyways.

Yesterday morning I went into the free clinic, just for a check up. I didn't want any more medical bills coming to the house— Steve doesn't need to worry about me and his Momma. I told the nurse what's been happening with my body. I've been throwing up a lot, my period is out of line, and I've had light cramps every day. I thought for sure it was stress, but after a few tests, I found out I'm pregnant. Before Momma's second leg went down river, Steve and I still managed to have a roll in the hay every now and then; mostly when Momma's ladies were over for cards. We went out to the cow fields down the road a ways in the pick-up truck. It wasn't glorious, but we both love each other, and that's a marital right neither of us wanted to give up.

The lady at the desk gave me a booklet on 'prenatal care.' I read the checklist inside on all the things I needed to do before the baby was even born. I stopped by the discount store to check on the vitamins and cribs I needed, and I started to cry when I saw the prices. Twenty dollars for a bottle of vitamins and two hundred for a crib that I didn't have room for. I only had three dollars in my purse. I thought maybe I could make a crib out of the bathtub; I could sit up against it and sleep. I'd be close when the baby cried. I sat down at the bus stop and the tears came again. Steve and I wouldn't be able to afford Momma and a baby. We couldn't even afford Momma, and I wanted Steve to be a daddy to our baby. He couldn't if he was always working. And having a baby screaming crying as Momma hollers about the noisy baby just after I gave birth, and getting even less sleep—she'd drive me insane. She'd drive me to… I just might…

I looked up at the sun and smiled. That was one year, seven months and nineteen days. That was yesterday.

Tonight marks the end of the twentieth day, and I am sitting with my husband in our living room on what I now think of as Momma's nasty bed. He's got his head on my shoulder and is crying his little baby tears like men do. I stroke his hair, lucky to have him off work and with me. I haven't seen him for three straight days.

"I feel so bad Steve. I thought Momma knew what she was doing. I had to go out for groceries, to get her favorite sugar free hard candy—"

"There's no need, honey. You tried to help Momma much as you possibly could. She must have just made a mistake and got some air into her needle, that's all."

"I'm so sorry, Steve."

"I feel like a bad son, because all I feel right now is sad and relief because she won't suffer anymore."

"I know."

I know the relief. I know the relief because I won't suffer Momma any more and I'll get my husband back and our baby won't suffer Momma either. And I made sure of that.

"From the series *Louisiana Stockyards*"

Beth Kleinpeter

An Ugly Work

Persephone Pontelier

It is an ugly work,
this hunt for affection.

We crawl along the walls of bars,
rubbing imprints in like your Yellow Wallpaper heroine,
building inside the walls enemies and lovers.

Tell him I'll be waiting on a bar stool,
maybe a vodka-tonic-or-two-too-many,
but inside of my seated sway
lies an open heart
ready to lock into a Möbius strip
of couch cuddles
and soft kisses
on puffy morning eyes.

"Gold"

Elise Toups

How To Be Like Dolly

Jade Benoit

Forget what they say about your body & arrange
your solid skeleton the way you like, check your makeup

in your wineglass. Stand on the porch & wield
your rifle at every beautiful bird saying, *I set out to get you*

with a fine-tooth comb. Sew a wig from your mama's
patchwork curtains. Select a bra big enough for your

ammunition, your grenades in the dance hall, bursting
with glittery nail polish & pennywhistles. At night, remove

your eyelashes & place them in a fruit jar beside the bed.
The moon will leak onto your birch floor, each piece

of light plucked like a banjo because your every chord
is loud, because you see yourself as flakes of paint

glued back to the plywood on an old house.
Iron your mink coat. Tomorrow, you're wearing it

to a cockfight. Remember your ragdolls are tiny
backwoods drag queens with names like *Wishy Washy Laundry*

& *Delta Dawn*. Remember your voice is the night sky
dressed in cigarette burns & you sing everything.

You cut things open & sing what's inside.

"What's the plan?"

Eva Mathews

On the Ignorance of Flowers

Sarah Howze

You called it a blackberry winter
        I've heard others say
                strawberry or dogwood winter as well.
Outside my window,
        the monstrosity of a fig tree
                has sets of perfect baby figs on it.
I woke to find them frozen—killed
        by five a.m.'s frost. *This is the*
                fairytale where all the young things die.
If you don't believe me,
        and I suspect you don't,
                I could show you the crime scene.
A picture of a young palm frond
        lime green and feathery soft
                shellacked in ice, glistening, crippled.
It is still winter you know,
        and this is no time for flowers, but
                all over uptown, the gardens are careless.
They have un-abashedly
        started the Easter Parade early,
                completely unaware of snapfrosts
                        that hang outside of February's door.

Imitating Fireflies

Kelly Jones

A Duke researcher spent her summers
recording glow patterns
and mating habits,
found that male bugs imitate females
so they can lure in other males to kill.

The boys on my cul-de-sac would swat
lightning bugs with baseball bats
as girls tried to catch fireflies
in jars half full of grass,
believing that would keep them alive longer.

Lightning bugs are not
as romantic or magical as they appear.
When a male kills another male he eats him.

The boys ripped off tails to smear
on the skin of the girl they liked best,
who'd go home glowing, knowing though they cried out
for the boys to stop, they still liked how cruelty felt,
loved the trails of light left behind.

Fireflies use bioluminescence for sexual selection,
they glow to let nearby bugs know they're ready.

The boys and the girls eventually lost
interest in lightning bugs.
Focused on each other instead,
shared cigarettes and stolen wine
in a park after curfew, two to a swing.

Some female bugs kill, not to mate, but just survive.
They shine the right light to attract males
and then feed on them.

The girls pretended to hate the hunt,
acted like the boys had to work for it,
had to say things like *aren't the lights in the sky beautiful*,
the boys not realizing they were there that night
only because the girls wished them to be.

"From the series *Louisiana Stockyards*"

Beth Kleinpeter

What To Say To A Bull After It Gores You

Erin Paige Grauel

He shot the bull four times through the eye. She did not hear the shots but she felt the quake in the huge body as it sank, pulling her forward on its head, so that she seemed, when Mr. Greenleaf reached her, to be bent over whispering some last discovery into the animal's ear.—Flannery O'Connor's *Greenleaf.*

I whisper to the bull, remove the horns-
They hurt my side. I like my ribs *sans* horns.
I hate to see the gifts of Adam torn.

He whispers back a question: "See the Light?"
I see the blood, I see the clay; no light.
"You're looking wrong," he says. "You have no sight."

You're lying, bull, quit talking all that noise.
I'm dead. Why don't I hear the trumpet noise?
I whisper to the bull, I want my boys.

I whisper to the bull, I want some peace.
I want some quiet time alone in peace.
I hate my farm, my life, my land, my lease.

The bull he whispers back, "Be quiet now
a moment full of grace is passing now."

Atop the Cultural Continental Divide

Stephanie Kadel Taras

Excerpted from the forthcoming book *Mountain Girls: What My Years in Appalachia Taught Me About Friendship, Creativity, and Living Life on My Own Terms*

On my drives from Ann Arbor, Michigan, to Elkins, West Virginia, I consider Zanesville, Ohio, my official gateway to the mountains. A curved iron bridge spans I-70 here, as it connects the two sides of a rock-faced gorge that hints at the elevation changes to come. After passing through more than three hours of flat Michigan and Ohio farmland—"former lake bottom," my husband explains— the shadowy gorge at Zanesville is comforting. I feel less exposed, better protected.

Soon I turn south toward the Ohio River, which forms the state border between Marietta, Ohio, and Parkersburg, West Virginia. Before I cross the steel truss bridge high over the wide, slow river, I always stop for fuel. Gas stations are not so numerous across the border.

Halfway over the bridge, I pass the sign of welcome to my home state. For a while around the turn of the millennium, the sign advertised a new state motto, "West Virginia: Open for Business." Every time I saw it, I couldn't help thinking of a reclining woman with her legs stretched wide, an invitation to be screwed over. Cynical locals revised it as "West Virginia: Hoping for Business."

I was relieved and delighted to discover around 2005 a reversion to the previous, oft-repeated motto: "Wild, Wonderful West Virginia." The residents I know really do embrace this description, but they're just as likely to say they're from "West By God Virginia." I like to think they mean it literally.

I exit at Parkersburg, and the high-speed interstate gives way to an empty four-lane cutting through increasingly looming hills. It's another three hours before the setting of my youth reveals itself to be tucked among some of the tallest peaks and deepest ravines of the state. The mountains emerge higher and closer here, more shady, wild, sheltering. I have to keep my car clear of weighty trucks on the long downhills. But I have trouble attending to the road as I pass familiar and welcome sights—cows grazing on absurdly steep hillsides, gravel driveways disappearing at impossible angles, clear water trickling right out of the cut-away rock, the "Welcome Home to Randolph County" sign decorated with rhododendron flowers and a fiddle.

I take the first Elkins exit off the new stretch of highway that has drawn a straight line between Elkins and the rest of the world. When I was a kid, the first and last hour of any road trip was slow going on a narrow, winding two-lane that was sure to make my car-sick sister green. Now the highway allows potential tourists and their pocketbooks to skip Elkins entirely, unimpeded by traffic lights, mom-and-pop restaurants, and actual fiddle players.

When I exit onto that familiar, old blacktop, I enter Elkins from the west, and soon encounter "The Mall," as the sign still reads out front of the town's first strip mall. It is now anchored by a four-screen movie theater and fast-food restaurants we would have died for as kids. Soon I come to Scottie's Diner, site of so many deep conversations of my youth.

Turning into downtown, I see the First United Methodist Church, where I sang duets with my sister and giggled with friends in the back row until old ladies turned around to shush us. And then I come upon my family's former house on First Street, with the tiny front yard my father paved for a parking spot, the wrap-around porch, and the rotting windows, half of which never did open. My parents are long gone from this place, transplanted to Florida in 1985.

I drive on to the other home where I spent much of my teenage years—the family home of my best friend Lisa. She lives in Baltimore now, working as a graphic designer, but we meet up at her mom's a couple of times a year. I pull my car into the drive behind Lisa's, turn off the engine, and breathe a sigh of relief. Good roads and cruise control get me into these once forbidding hills in a matter of hours. And as I look toward the horizon at the ridges surrounding my hometown, I feel safer here, as if the outside world can't get to me now. Whatever was worrying me before I left Ann Arbor feels impotent here.

It must be the same feeling early settlers had, squatting on land they thought no one else would bother with, or moonshiners during

Prohibition, hiding their stills in a gulch. The promise of seclusion lulls me into a kind of complacency that is as dangerously false as it is addictive. After all, problems aren't impeded by geography, and I know mine have followed me here, just as Lisa's have followed her. But for a little while, at least, we will embrace and tell dog stories and eat home cooked food and pretend nothing can get us in these mountains.

As kids, we rued the mountainous terrain for keeping popular culture somewhat at bay. We wanted a McDonald's and better FM radio reception and cable TV. Many years later, the mountains would also delay reliable Internet and cell phone reception well into the Information Age.

But a lack of accessibility did not equate to a backward attitude about progress. When Hardee's, the town's first real fast-food restaurant opened in the early 1980s, it was standing-room-only for months. Nobody talked about obesity epidemics back then, and Elkins's initial love affair with Hardee's was not a sad commentary on the eating habits of the impoverished and unenlightened. Everybody in Elkins—rich and poor, educated and illiterate, rednecks and town folks—wanted to get their hands on those sausage biscuits, greasy burgers, and salty fries. And few seemed to bat an eye that the building of the Hardee's franchise required tearing down a historic brick house on the main drag. In hindsight, of course, the opening of Hardee's was like the arrival of the first small pox virus in North America (now that West Virginians are often cited as one of the fattest populations in the world), but at the time we thought of it as proof that we were coming up in society. We showed our appreciation for what others took for granted.

After the novelty wore off and the crowds dispersed, Hardee's became Lisa's and my favorite hangout. We sat across from each other in the plastic booth, dipping fries into a shared cup of ketchup. Lisa dipped her cheeseburger into the ketchup, too.

"Let's buy high-top tennis shoes for school this year," she said.

"You mean boys' shoes?" I asked.

"You know, Chuck Taylors. Like they wear to play basketball.

It'll be cool."

"I don't have any money," I said.

"Your parents have to buy you shoes for school."

I shrugged. Lisa bought hers first. She had already started drawing on them when she came to show me.

"You want those?" my father said in the shoe store, looking at my feet. I had gone to the boys section and found a size three pair of cream-colored canvas high-tops with red and blue trim. They didn't make Chuck Taylors for girls yet, nor did they have any creative colors. I had pulled them onto my feet, laced them up my ankles, and stomped over to a mirror. After years of church shoes, boat shoes, and cheap sneakers, these felt like steel-toed work boots. I was immediately more sure of myself, ass-kicking confident. They were right. Lisa was so right.

My father was incredulous. "You'll wear them the first day, kids will laugh at you, and you'll never wear them again." It wasn't like him to express an opinion about my clothes, but this was the only money he had to spend on school shoes for the year.

"No I won't, Dad," I whined. "I like them. I'll wear them every day. I promise."

And I did. I cut my jeans short at the shin to show them off. I cut my hair short and spikey to add to the effect. The popular girls who had liked me in junior high stopped hanging out with me. "What happened to Stephanie over the summer?" I heard whispered once in the hall. I didn't care. I had high-tops. I had Lisa.

I've been telling people in Michigan about my recent trips to West Virginia to reconnect with my hometown, my old friends, and new stories of old places.

"Hope you have a great trip to Virginia," says a woman who has known me for years.

"How was Virginia?" asks another woman upon my return to Ann Arbor. We're shopping at Zingerman's Deli—Ann Arbor's coolest and priciest fancy food store.

"I was in *West* Virginia," I say, as I dip a piece of baguette in a tasting cup of extra virgin olive oil. I know that correcting people's minor mistakes in conversation is awkward and unkind, but I do try to clarify "*West* Virginia" when they get it wrong. I can't figure out if most people have never heard that one of the fifty states is called West Virginia, if they don't see the need to distinguish between the two states, or if they just can't believe that's the place I mean.

If it sinks in that I'm talking about a different state from Virginia, and which state that is, their faces suddenly change like they're thinking, "You grew up in that place of inbred hicks and barefoot children and black lung? How did you make it out of there?" Maybe, as we're standing together buying aged balsamic vinegar and cocoa-dusted almonds, it's easier for them to imagine me growing up in Richmond or Norfolk or Alexandria.

West Virginia writer John O'Brien describes having the same experiences during the years he and his wife lived outside of the state. He found that while people often didn't know anything about West Virginia, or thought he was talking about western Virginia, they did know about Appalachia and the images of poverty and hillbillies the term tends to conjure. He deemed such conversations an "odd confusion in the background of our lives."

When I have tried to bring clarity to such confusion, some people simply wave off the distinction between West Virginia and Virginia. The *West* doesn't seem to register at all, like I just tried to distinguish between Roquefort and bleu cheese. I want to point out that West Virginia *seceded* from Virginia and really doesn't have anything to do with that other state of urban riches, Atlantic coastline, and southern charm. But I don't know if I should remind them of the Civil War, when West Virginia managed to become its own state but never seemed to embrace its Yankee status.

If you look at a topographical map, you'll see that Elkins is tucked away in the heart of the Allegheny Mountains that run through eastern West Virginia. As part of the larger Appalachian Mountain range, the Alleghenies are host to the Eastern Continental Divide, separating watersheds that run east to the Atlantic Ocean from watersheds that run west to the Mississippi and Gulf of Mexico. As a child, I didn't know I lived at an apex between east and west, but I always knew I lived somewhere between the north and the south. In seventh grade, we were forced to take West Virginia history—in a junior high school building located on Robert E. Lee Avenue. I don't remember learning much of anything in that class. I certainly didn't learn why Elkins would have a street named after a Confederate general, if I even learned who Lee was.

I did the assignments well enough that the teacher invited me to write an essay on "Why We Study History" for some statewide competition where the winners would go to the state capital, Charleston, to observe a legislative session. She asked me and a boy named Mike to step out into the hall where she told us about the contest. (Mike and I were lab partners in science class, too; smart kids have to stick together if they want to learn anything.) I was thrilled to be tapped for this opportunity and excited about the possibility of winning. But when it came to the essay itself, I couldn't think of anything wise to say. I remember walking down the sidewalk in my neighborhood, really pondering the question, "Why *do* we study history?"

I had no idea. No adult I asked seemed to have an answer for me. I ended up writing a piece about the value of learning from our mistakes. I knew it was trite. I didn't win. (I don't remember if Mike did.) I think I've been pondering that question ever since.

Looking back now, the only thing I remember learning from West Virginia history class was the names of all the counties in the state, in alphabetical order. We were required to memorize and recite them: "Barbour, Berkeley, Boone, Braxton…" (I can't do it anymore; I had to look those up.)

Many years later, I met someone outside the state who could recite that list. When I was studying for my Ph.D. at Syracuse University, my professor of educational philosophy was a woman who grew up in Huntington, West Virginia. She had also been required to memorize the counties in alphabetical order, and thirty years later, she could still name them. She would do so at faculty parties or sometimes in class whenever the topic would arise of why schools teach such useless facts to students. She was dismayed that her own brain cells were still wasting space on that list.

My fellow West Virginia history students and I must have also learned somebody's interpretation of how West Virginia became a state, because as adults we all explain it the same way: the people living in western Virginia did not want to secede from the Union at the start of the Civil War, so we split from eastern and southern Virginia, formed our own state, and fought for the north. Right?

Well, sort of.

According to West Virginia historian John Alexander Williams, the first white settlers in this area, who came prior to the Revolutionary War, were looking for land to farm and hunt and feed their families. They found upland glades with meadows for grazing animals, springs coming out of the hillsides for water, level hilltops for sparse crops, and dense forests for hunting small game. "Convenient indeed for the man of modest ambition," writes Williams.

The state was created by men of greater ambition. West Virginia was not birthed by mountaineers fighting against Old Dominion plantation owners, but by western Virginia elites who were recreating their own antebellum culture, mirroring their neighbors to the south and east, but on smaller farms with fewer slaves. They felt underrepresented by decisions made in Richmond which granted voting rights only to white men with substantial land holdings. Conflicts between western Virginians and eastern Virginians raged for decades before the Civil War furnished an opportunity to settle the matter.

Such regional identities within one state were hardly uncommon in other states before the Civil War, and it was no more severe in nineteenth century Virginia than it still is today in places like northern and southern California or upstate and downstate New York. But the Civil War heightened the divide. When Virginia voted on May 23, 1861, to secede from the Union, western Virginians had already held a pro-Union convention in Wheeling. And in October, residents in thirty-nine western Virginia counties voted to form a new Unionist state. Whether the vote accurately represented the wishes of the majority of residents is hard to know, since Union troops were already in the area and were stationed at polls to keep out Confederate sympathizers.

The divide was further solidified by the war itself. For two years, a military line crossed the region, separating the Union-held northwest from the confederate capital at Richmond and its surroundings. Due to bad weather, steep mountain roads, and mud, neither side could be assured a victory if it tried to move from its encampments. Lincoln assigned Union generals to this front who were owed a political favor but could not be trusted to handle more challenging military duties.

Meanwhile, the elites in western Virginia convened to develop a new state constitution and called themselves the Restored Government of Virginia. Lincoln recognized this body as the legitimate government of Virginia and welcomed new senators and congressmen to Washington. Since the U.S. Constitution says a new state must gain approval from the original state, the Restored Government granted permission to itself to form the state of West Virginia. When the U.S. Senate approved a statehood proposal on July 14, 1862, West Virginia, the 35th state, became the only successful secession of the Civil War. It may not have been God's doing, but West By God Virginia was a done deal.

Williams claims that the "subterfuge" upon which the state was founded has endured to this day in "an apologetic posture, a defensiveness that made West Virginians overly eager for friendly national attention and for outsiders' approval but overly sensitive to bad publicity and criticism."

When I read this last passage, I underlined it and starred it three times in the margin. Here was an explanation for my defensiveness with my Michigan friends, for my desire to be recognized as West Virginian, and for some of the drive to write about my home state. One hundred and fifty years after the state's creation, so many generations removed from the Civil War that most Americans don't know much of the story, West Virginians like me are still trying to justify ourselves, and the rest of the country maintains a shoulder-shrugging indifference to our existence. I never cease to be amazed at how human society passes down attitudes like genetic code.

But what about the fact that my junior high school was built on Robert E. Lee Avenue? Or that southern accents and sausage gravy flow freely among the folks of West Virginia?

History has revealed that the people of this region were by no means in agreement on the matter of separating, or even particularly opposed to southern priorities. After all, the new state's constitution did not outlaw slavery or free the slaves living there. And when the war started, many young men left their homes in western Virginia to join with the Rebels. If they were lucky enough to return after the war, they found themselves living in a new state.

Consider Stonewall Jackson. When I was a teenager, I went to a weekend church camp every fall at Jackson's Mill, a historic property near Weston, West Virginia, that belonged to the family of Stonewall Jackson. A huge portrait of this famous soldier in his Confederate uniform hung over the fireplace in the dark meeting hall, looking down on us campers as we ate spaghetti at long wood tables. West Virginians continue to honor him as their own, because he was born in Clarksburg and grew up at Jackson's Mill. But Stonewall Jackson always considered himself a loyal Virginian. During the war, he begged to be transferred back to his home territory to roust the Unionists from what had become West Virginia.

Today, West Virginians celebrate Stonewall Jackson and other vestiges of southern heritage without any apparent identity crisis. It's as if they dare outsiders to say they can't be both loyalist and rebel. Why can't they have southern charm and northern hospitality, southern grit and northern wit? Having it both ways means they don't have to accept either way. They can simply be a unique people, somewhere between, not of, the north or the south. Wild *and* wonderful. Hip holy rollers. Refined rednecks. Living atop the Cultural Continental Divide.

When I was a child, I jealously guarded my state from Yankees who called it southern. Long before I understood the social, historical, and political identities of the South, long before I knew much about the Civil War, I was a staunch defender of West Virginia to outsiders from farther north. I thought the weather would demonstrate the difference. "We aren't southern," I used to say. "It's too cold. School is always being called off for snow days." Perhaps I felt that paying the dues of harsh winters gave me the bragging rights of a northerner.

But I had no particular sense of a northern identity, either. I simply always wanted to be West Virginian. And I wanted others to see that West Virginians were not what those outsiders imagined. We didn't all go barefoot and have coal mines in our backyards as some kid at a camp in New York asked my sister. We ate fast food and listened to cool music and bought Chuck Taylors if we wanted them. As a teenager, I was awakening to what the rest of the world thought of my beloved state, but I wasn't ready then to stand up for its unique culture. I wanted to prove we were just like everybody else.

A few years ago, I was watching television at home in Ann Arbor the day Martha Stewart was released from a prison in West Virginia. I noticed that every time the news media mentioned her prison stay, they always noted its location. Do you think they would have done that if the prison had been in New York? (Of course, even if the media had repeatedly said it was in New York, no New Yorker would have cared.) But I think it sounded to the reporters like extra punishment to send the queen of hand-made wreaths and elegant table settings to serve her time in unclean, backward West Virginia, where Martha was appalled to discover she couldn't get a fresh lemon.

Today, I purposely tell people I'm from West Virginia because I like how it sounds. Although being a native-born Floridian is in itself unusual, there's nothing much interesting about saying I'm from Florida or from Michigan. I like being from somewhere unexpected and unfamiliar. It's the same mystique about West Virginia that other people disdain that makes me proud—and therefore complicit in rendering West Virginia abnormal. Similarly, I want to use the state to hide from outsiders while simultaneously ensuring that West Virginia is acknowledged by them. No wonder everyone else is confused.

I went to a conference recently in Baltimore for people who, like me, write family histories for a living. They came from all over the U.S. and Canada and a few other countries. They were a sensitive bunch—kind, nonjudgmental, good listeners, accepting of all walks of life—as you would expect of professionals who interview people about their most personal stories.

One morning during the danish and coffee conference break-fast, I found myself sitting next to a handsome young man from England. Our conversation began innocuously enough with him asking where I grew up.

"West Virginia," I said. "Just a few hours west of here, actually." I expected the usual Virginia confusion, especially from someone who wasn't from this country. But he surprised me.

"Is it true what I've heard about West Virginia?" His British accent dripped like honey onto scones. "Families feuding and people living away in the mountains working in coal mines?"

I wanted to give a thoughtful answer, one that recognized the origins of stereotypes but spoke to the depth and breadth of the population and its cultures. My mind flashed from a review of the state's industries, to a description of rich mountain traditions, to the realities of modern corporate culture that has homogenized even the hardest to reach hollers. I opened my mouth and got out "Well…" when another woman to the left of the Brit jumped in. Her name tag said she was from Minneapolis.

"It's true!" she said with breathless excitement. "I knew a woman from down where those Hatfields and McCoys lived, and she said they were all like that." His eyes widened. "It's dangerous down there." The bloke was caught up in her dramatic tale and turned his body to face her. She went on, but I couldn't listen anymore.

I'm sitting in my home office when the phone rings. I can see on the caller ID that Lisa is calling. Even though I'm anxious for new clients to call, I'm relieved to see it's just her.

I pick it up and say, "Hey."

"Hey. Guess what? I got my passport in the mail today."

"Excellent."

Lisa is planning her first international trip, and it is her first ever passport. I'm excited about her plans to see Europe with some friends. I've been twice to Europe, once as a child with my mother and once for a semester in college, so I've had a passport since I was eleven.

"So I opened the passport," she says, "and guess what they have as my state of birth?"

"Oh no."

"Virginia!"

We laugh—a familiar, despairing laugh. We've heard this joke before.

"Chicken"

Merçedes Jelinek

The Trains Don't Roar Like They Used To

Kelly Jones

This town grew up out of the railroads. The highest stop
on the old Chatham line where people got off to start farms, families.

By the time I was born Apex was just a suburb of Raleigh.
Growing up I watched the woods disappear, saw the highways come in.

I walked to school: up a hill, across the tracks, past four churches.
Sometimes a stalled train blocked the way and I had to climb through it.

Lifting myself up the rusty ladder I would pray the train
wouldn't start moving. Then I'd look around at the town, pray it would.

"Cowgirls"

Jenilee Domingue

Feet

Liz Hogan

(A nursery rhyme)

I was born with crooked feet
feet turned in like prayer
sure, I was a baby once
could still fly through the air.

Soon though, these feet grew flat
took me out upon the land
kissed the dirt, the earth and grass
felt the singing dance of sand.

And on my walks, I caught the thought:
this world still longs to fly
but give 'em wings
they'll ask for feet
and sure, a chance to die.

"Squish"

Eva Mathews

Excerpt from "The Last Whistle"

Gladys Cagle Tritico Stoker

Plum trees shaded the beehives
and could have been pretty good
for the honey works

but papa's bees preferred locust nectar
from the trees across the road
in a rich man's pasture.

Our bees were hob-nobbing
from the very first
like papa's kids turned out.

Well, we didn't mean for it
to turn out that way.
We just felt better around money,

of which there was absolutely none
in our house or
buried in our yard.

So we launched out
as soon as we got old enough,
hunting locust trees

in a rich man's pasture,
when plum nectar
would have been better.

"From the series *Louisiana Stockyards*"

Beth Kleinpeter

Five Year Plan

Lynda Lou Plunkett

Everybody's makin a five year plan
You got to tighten up
Plot the course
Graduate
Get married
Then get divorced
You got to keep your house clean
And iron all your clothes
Keep your car clean
So that no body knows
Your mind aint clean
Your soul aint clean
Your conscience, it aint clean
And what about your heart?

"Sister Regis' Funeral"

AP

Hurricanes

Andi Malisheski

My dear, the sun is out;

Let's you and I become a storm

And with our fingers push them all about

The sea, those creatures of the deep which form

A dizzy dream until it is our wont to sleep.

The stars have crowned your head, your

Eyes are winking clouds below your brow,

The moon. Four windy arms will smooth the shore about,

East, West, North, South: A bed of sand—until we laugh and blow

Our tiny lighthouse candles out.

And, crashing there, we sigh

And grow still; until—until

In our death we share a living breath, and as we die

This hurricane is you and I.

"One Light On Moore Hill"

Alicia Hartfield

What You Came In With

Cynthia Williams

She preferred to sing her stories
—not much of a reader—
hummed wild and lived out
of the clothes basket, measuring no
teaspoons and feeding scores.

In another life he wrote novels
and Baldwin was my daddy.
Here, he survived basic training, in him
grandpa's preacher dreams
dormant then busy like shingles.

Meaning business, she tended
to the children, the neighbors, him
(who hibernated from just about all, from
making choices, groundhogging now and
then to quote scripture, to close

all those windows she'd opened, knew
sin came in with the sun)
in the kitchen where she threw
down. They'd dance. His plate
heaped up, and her appreciated.

"Whitney"

Molly Gardner

If The Devil Don't Catch Her

Janey Hogan

He has a demon and is insane, why listen to him? – John 10:20

Two uncertain stilettos stumbled across a dark path that led to a stone bench thoughtfully placed beneath a giant oak tree. Louise De Mahy kicked off her borrowed shoes and draped herself, belly up, with more weariness than grace, upon the warm stone. She heaved the sigh of an exhausted maid of honor who spent the past three days catering to a highly Catholic southern Louisiana bride. Louise lit her first cigarette of the night and inhaled slowly as she twirled her ankles in circles.

"Well, well, if it isn't my wife? Fancy seeing you here."

Although he approached soundlessly from the shadows, his presence did not startle Louise. She knew this encounter was inevitable ever since she discovered his name on the RSVP list. She exhaled with tense annoyance, "Don't call me that."

"Oh my darling," he smirked, "Have you really had so much to drink that you don't remember marrying me? You do know our marriage is legal until *we* end it. That means you're still technically mine."

She bolted upright and glared at the man who was delighted by her discomfort, "I am not your technical anything, Henri. Jesus. Can you really not see me in public without causing a scene?"

"Maybe I can't," his eyes glittered a medicated insanity that made her skin crawl, "You're too fucking beautiful, you know that?"

"I'm going inside." She placed her barely rested feet onto the ground, crushed out her cigarette and snatched up her shoes. As she walked away from him, she glanced his way but did not hold his gaze, "You got no kinda spine, Henri Stanton."

The Caribbean sun poured out of a cloudless sky and onto the sleepy Mexican village of Bacalar, where a few dozen wooden huts cluster on the edge of a crystal green *Laguna*. For nearly a week the town was buzzing from fresh gossip of the activities of the American couple who had checked into the town's only guesthouse. They were not married, and he spoke no Spanish. They brought beer into their room at night and laughed loudly until dawn. They would emerge at noon and play cards on their balcony over coffee and cigarettes. They swam every few hours, making the short pilgrimage from their room to the *Laguna*. The girl wore a black bikini and the man kept his t-shirt on at all times. She skipped, sometimes ran to the water, shrieking with delight as she jumped in, surfacing to call out to the man who had not once quickened his pace,

"*¡Henri! ¡Está frío, amor!*"

He would smile and reply, "You know I don't know what you're saying."

In the evenings they would stroll, arm in arm, through the narrow dusty road of Bacalar. She would lean her head on his shoulder and declare every house they passed a potential new home.

"Look, Henri! The porch is so charming! Let's offer them a million pesos right now for it and move in tomorrow! We can play chess and drink cocktails on the porch....or fuck it, Henri! We don't need the house, let's just live right on this porch!"

Henri replied that he would buy the entire block if it made her happy, provided he would never be forced to spend a night there.

One night they strolled through the market. He loved the way she crowed with happiness over the slightest of trinkets.

"It's divine!"

"It's a hammock, my dear."

"Nooooo!" She caught his eye and flashed a playful grin, "This is a *chinchorro*, Henri Stanton!"

"Oh, is it, my dear?" He returned her smile as their game began, "Well, please Miss De Mahy, enlighten me on the difference between a hammock and a *chin-chongo*?"

"It's a well-known fact that hammocks are made out of cloth, and *chinchorros* are woven from nylon. And it's a little-known fact that this one right here is the most perfect *chinchorro* in the entire world!"

"And what makes this *chinchorro* so extraordinary, my love?"

She stared deep into his eyes with a look he could not yet read. She leaned in and whispered into his ear, "Because it's here and because we are seeing it."

He smiled, although he did not understand. "Darling, let me buy you this *chinchorro*."

She laughed, "Henri, what the fuck am I gonna do with a *chinchorro*?"

They strolled to the plaza and settled on a bench beneath a palm tree. She leaned her head on his shoulder, and she sighed happily, "Life feels so perfect right now."

He held her hand and said, "I'll make every day perfect for you, darling."

"*¡Helado! ¡Helado! ¡Helado!*" A jingle of bells approached them, and Henri was annoyed to see a younger man pushing an ice cream cart.

She bolted upright, "*Uno de coco, por favor*, do you want one Henri?"

"I'm fine, darling," he automatically reached into his pocket and handed the ice cream seller a ten peso note.

The ice cream seller grinned and produced a coconut ice cream pop, "*¿De dónde son?*" [Where are you from?]

"*Los Estados Unidos.*" [The United States]

"*Él también?*" [Him as well?]

"*Sí, pero somos de partes diferentes.*" [Yes, but we're from different parts.]

"*Sí nota, mamí. ¿De dónde son, usted?*" [I can tell, *mamí*. What part are you from?]

"*Soy del surrr, surr, el parte mas sur de los Estados,*" she grinned "*De los pantanos acercita de Nueva Orleans.*" [I'm from the soouuuuth, the most south of the states, I'm from the swamps around New Orleans.]

"*¡Ah! Nueva Orleans que chido, ¿y él?*" [Ah! New Orleans, cool! And him?]

"*Noo, che, él es un Yankee de Nueva York.*" [He's a Yankee, homie, from New York.]

He laughed at her Spanish and was puzzled over the blank look of her companion.

"*¿Ah, él no habla español?*" [Ah, he doesn't speak Spanish?]

"*Ni, una palabra.*" [Not a single word.]

During this repartee Henri shifted in his seat half a dozen times. He suffered from bipolar and acute anxiety disorders, which were kept in check with heavy medication. Unfamiliar situations did not thrill his heart, but she did.

He stared impatiently at the intruder, "Hey, no hab-low espan-yol, compañero! I'm sorry, could you leave us alone now?"

The young man's face fell as he instantly remembered that he sold ice cream for a living. He glanced with humiliation at Louise and mumbled, "*Me disculpes.*" [Please excuse me.]

After he walked off, Louise's mouth fell open, "What the *fuck* was that? That was so rude, Henri!"

"Well, I'm sorry, I can't help it that you're so beautiful, and every guy in Mexico wants to fuck you."

"He didn't want to fuck me; I was tellin' him where we're from."

"Darling, I'm sorry, what I meant to say is that you're so beautiful, and I want you all to myself."

She frowned and fumbled in her bag for a cigarette.

"Louise."

"Yeah?"

He grabbed her hand and stared into her eyes, "Will you marry me? Right here – in this church? Before God and before Mexico….. will you? Please Louise. I need to make you my wife."

Her eyebrows knitted in bewilderment, "Why? You've only known me three weeks."

"I was put on this earth to be with you. I thought you felt the same."

"I doooo…" her voice trailed off as she stuck a cigarette in between her lips.

Within a split second, Henri produced a Dunhill lighter from his pocket. He lit her cigarette with the smooth maneuver of a middle-aged man whose life was sponsored by an inexhaustible trust fund. This made him an expert at lighting cigarettes, mixing exotic cocktails, speaking about the opera, and ordering expensive entrees. Until Henri, no man had ever opened a car door for Louise De Mahy, let alone paid for her dinner. She was accustomed to taking care of complicated southern men with drinking problems. All of the men from her past had been so angry at her and at the world, no matter how softly she treated them. As she watched the shiny lighter disappear, Louise remembered how easy life had been since she met Henri and how easy her future could be.

He crouched in front of her and softly took her hand, "Let's get married, in this church, right now. Please?"

Her sun lit eyes stared at him for a long moment. He had dark hair, long eyelashes and freckles across a beautiful bone structure. Louise admired his face and forgot about the ice cream vendor. Her green eyes flashed with the clinical mania that created a three week love affair; now on its third country and fifth marriage proposal. Perhaps Louise De Mahy's impeccable ability at getting herself out of trouble was the exact reason she fell into it with so much ease.

"Fuck it." She whispered and smiled like a mad dog, "Let's do it. Right here, in this church."

Louise had eagerly awaited a day she could bring Henri to her family's stilted camp on the edge of the Bogue Chitto River. She spoke frequently about the camp, calling it her favorite place in the entire world. She gave him a two minute tour of the property, displaying each room with a simple proudness.

"Here's the kitchen and the bathroom, and these are the bunk beds where my sisters and I slept when we were little, and look here's a chalkboard that we used to play school whenever it rained..."

Henri pulled Louise close to him and kissed her. "Where will we be sleeping?"

"Hold on, Henri, I'm giving you the tour."

"I want to take a tour of you."

She laughed the same strained and distant laugh that developed since their arrival from Mexico. Henri constantly said and did things that Louise found obnoxious or strange. It made him less handsome in her eyes and she often thought of other things while he was on top of her.

"Let's wait, I want a drink first."

Henri excused himself to the bathroom and dry swallowed two Xanax pills from the stash in his pocket. He was relieved that the pills would ease the insecurity and sadness that his marriage now brought. When they returned from Mexico, Louise stopped laughing at his jokes. She laughed at the television, at books she read, and at jokes told by others. But she no longer laughed, and rarely smiled, at Henri. He tried so hard to talk with her, to begin games of jest and jeer that would result in the deep laughter they shared in Latin America. But his beautiful wife refused to jest in return. She would blink into space with a look that told Henri she had sent her mind away to linger on memories and thoughts that did not concern him.

He left the bathroom and found Louise on the deck, smoking a cigarette and gazing at the full moon.

"I made you a drink."

He took a sip of a perfectly mixed gin and tonic. "This is delicious darling, thank you."

She smiled absently, "I'm so glad we decided to come, Henri. Just wait till you see the river in the morning. It's so peaceful."

He smiled and drank his drink, not knowing what to say. He numbly reached for her hand, which she allowed him to hold.

Their moment of silence was broken by an alarm sounding in the distance.

"What the fuck is that?"

"I don't know boo, it's not anybody's house. I mean nobody puts an alarm like that on a camp."

"Well, what the fuck is it?"

"Henri, whatever it is its fine."

"We need to call the cops."

"What do you mean, the cops? What are they gonna do? The alarm company is already calling the cops, that's not on us."

"I can't believe I'm hearing this from you. Have you lost your fucking mind? We gotta call the cops Louise!"

"Henri, boo," she squeezed his hand "Just calm down."

He jerked his hand away, "See Louise, for times like this you need a fucking gun."

"Oh my god, are you serious?"

"We are so exposed right here."

"From what? My lord, there's nothing tryin to get us!"

"Shut up, we're not talking about this now Louise. I'm going to close the gate and then we're calling the cops."

She burst into laughter.

"What the fuck? I don't think this is funny! Stop laughing."

"Oh!" she gasped, "I just can't help it – you're being ridiculous!"

"Louise, for fucks sake this is serious."

She composed herself, "Ok, ok, you do what you think you gotta. Go close the gate boo, but bring Suki with you." Suki looked up from the floor at the mention of her name and stretched as she rose.

"Louise, I'm going to lock the gate. You are going to go inside and lock the door and not answer it for anyone except me."

She erupted into snickers. He put his hands on her shoulders and shook her, "Listen! What are you going to do?"

"Oh lord, I'm going to go inside and lock the fucking door and not open it for anybody but you."

"The password is Rainwater, I'll shout it as I approach."

"Do you really think this is necessary?"

He pressed his lips to hers in a spongy dry-mouthed kiss and headed down the porch calling, "Louise! Go inside now!"

She went inside chuckling at the thought of calling the police. There was no address to the camp, there was no postal service, and it wasn't on any trash route. Louise lit a cigarette and thought of the hilarious directions she would give the police operator, "Well, you turn left at the store, you pass the cemetery, you keep straight, before you reach the chicken houses you veer off and follow the river till you get to the driveway on your left….can't miss it!"

The alarm pounded into Henri's ears as he raced through the woods in a state of utter paranoia. Suki chased his heels and he cursed himself for leaving New Orleans without a weapon. His fingers trembled as he closed the rusted metal gate. The alarm abruptly ceased and Henri knew in his heart this meant the thieves had reached the De Mahy camp and were initiating a gang bang of Louise.

Henri began to run full speed back to the camp. He prayed that the lock held firm and it would buy Louise some time before the cops showed up. The lock was his saving grace and the only thing that separated his wife from the rabid rapists.

In his haste he forgot to shout Rainwater. He bounded up the stairs two at a time, and put his hand on the door handle calling, "Sweetheart, it's me, it's Henri…open up –"

The door opened without effort, it was unlocked. Louise was lounging in a wicker chair smoking a cigarette and strumming through a National Geographic.

"Hey boo, there's this tribe in the outermost region of Zimbabwe that has no concept of time and ---"

She jumped as Henri slammed the door and shouted, "Are you trying to prove a point?"

"Excuse me?" she whispered.

"Not locking the door, is this your way of saying 'Fuck you Henri I'll let myself get murdered and raped!' Huh? You selfish little bitch!"

His voice was angry and accusatory and his eyes were wild. He approached her like a lion would approach a mouse.

Louise's inner alarm went off and her mind raced: *Holy shit, he has it in him. He was supposed to be.....how could I not see this?*

"Whoa, whoa...." She began to chant softly and shook her head.

Henri stalked towards her, with a crazy smile twisted across his beautiful mouth. "You fucking whore....."

"I didn't do anything, Henri! I didn't, I--"

He advanced toward her quickly and she began to tremble. She knew this situation all too well and it meant that she should run fast.

Unfortunately for Louise De Mahy, she had nowhere to run.

Henri came down with traveler's diarrhea his first night in Managua. After he missed two full days of classes, his roommate insisted that he get some broth soup in the food market by the hotel. Market food sounded much more appealing than the hotel's fish, which Henri blamed for his stomach problems. While Jake was in class, Henri hobbled across the road to the market.

The table was wooden and dirty and his waitress was eleven.

"*¿Que queires, señor?*" [What would you like, mister?]

"Umm no hablo, no, fuck, I don't speak Spanish. Look I just want some soup alright? Soup?" He formed his hands into a bowl.

The young girl nodded, "*¿Ah, ok, sopa? ¿Queires sopa?*" [Ah, ok, soup? You want soup?]

"Yes! Sí! Sopa ok! And a coca cola!"

"*Una sopa y una coca cola – a la orde.*" [One soup and one coca cola, coming right up.]

She walked away and he heard a laugh from a table at the next stall over.

Henri turned to face a striking woman, with long dark curls, thin limbs, and giant black sunglasses that covered her face. He decided she was too tall to be a Nicaraguan and must be Argentinean. She was clutching an enormous novel, sipping a delicious looking smoothie, and she was laughing at him.

"What's so funny?"

"Ha! You! Attempting to mime out what you wanted to eat. Just think if you had wanted to order chicken." She grinned and flapped imaginary wings.

"I'm sorry, do I know you? Did I invite you to comment on my life?"

"No. But you talk loud and I'm the only one here that understood what you were saying so it sorta became my business. So, no, I wasn't invited but I don't feel bad commenting on this tiny moment of your life." The girl smiled and lit a cigarette. She was an American with a neutral accent.

Henri was insulted and fascinated. "What kinda person just sits by herself, smoking Marlboro Reds while everyone around her is eating? You're in some shitty market in Managua and you feel entitled to make fun of people for not knowing Spanish?"

"What asshole comes to a shitty market and doesn't bother to learn the word for soup?"

They stared hard at each other. He broke the silence. "Do you mind if I join you?"

"They do," she nodded to the watchful women stirring pots of *frijoles* and *caldos*. "You're in Dona Leti's kitchen, I'm in Veronica's, but I'll explain."

She sang some Spanish out to the old woman bringing Henri's soup. The woman replied and the girl grabbed her smoothie and book and deposited herself across from Henri.

"So what are you reading?"

She showed him the front.

"Cervantes, huh? How's that going?"

"It's not. It's one of those books that intelligent people are supposed to love and so by hating it you all of a sudden feel less intelligent."

"Like Shakespeare."

"Exactly. What are you reading?"

"Just a copy of *The New Yorker*."

"Well that's a shame."

"It's actually a fantastic magazine, have you ever tried to read it?"

She pushed back her chair, "I have to get going."

"I've bored you."

"I don't get bored…I just elect to change my scenery."

He looked down into his soup.

"I'm sorry, don't feel bad, I only really talked to you because I thought you were sick."

"I am sick."

She sank back into her chair, "Oh damn, boo….are you?" He now detected her accent. She was southern. "I'm so sorry, what you got?"

"Just diarehha and vomiting for the past two days."

"Mmm hmm, food or water poisoning no doubt. Did you go to a pharmacy?"

"This is the first time I've left my room since I arrived. Anyway, I haven't seen a doctor so there'd be no use in going to a pharmacy."

"Oh no, no, no. Go to a pharmacy. It's not like the States. You don't need a prescription to get drugs here."

His ears perked up, his eyebrows raised, and color returned to his cheeks, "Really? What kind of drugs?"

"Antiboitics and just about everything else."

"Like painkillers?"

She rolled her eyes, "Yeah American boy, like painkillers."

By the time he finished his soup, and before he ever asked for her name, Henri had convinced the stranger that he was morbidly ill and she agreed to accompany him to the pharmacy.

As they strolled through the pharmacy door, the girl called out "¡*Buuuenas!*" Henri slunk behind her and clutched his arm. A pretty older woman in a crisp white pharmacist coat smiled at them,

"*Hola Buenas tardes, ¿qué puede ayudar?*" [Good afternoon, how can I help you?]

"*Mira,*" the couple propped up on the glass counter and the girl did all the talking, "*Esta muchacho está muuuy mal ahora – tiene un infección del estomacho, está vomitando, tiene diarrehha, de todos. Necessita un antibiotic o no se, ¿que me recomendas?*" [Look, this guy is reaally sick right now. He has a stomach infection, he's vomiting, he has diarrhea, everything. He needs an antibiotic or, I'm not sure, what would you recommend?]

The pharmacist was slightly aghast by the bluntness of the girl's Spanish and turned her attention towards Henri.

"*Hola señor, digame lo que sienta por favor.*" [Hello Sir, please tell me how you're feeling.]

The girl interjected, "*No, no, linda, él no entiendo el español.*" [No, no *linda*, he doesn't understand Spanish.]

"*Ah, perdón, es que—*" [Oh, I'm sorry, it's just--]

"*Sí, sí, él parece Latino, pero no es.*" [Yeah, yeah, he looks Latino, but he isn't.]

"*¿De dónde viene?*" [Where's he from?]

"*De los Estados, pero no sé que parte – un Yankee por supesto.*" [The States, but I don't know which part. He's clearly a Yankee.]

"*¿Su novio?*" [Your boyfriend?]

"*¡Noooo! Apenas conocimos.*" [Nooo! We just met!]

The pharmacist chuckled, she liked the young girl, with her dark freckles and wild hair and the manner in which she jerked her body about in order to emhasize a word in Spanish.

"What'd you tell her?"

"Nothin, just that your stomach's all fucked."

The pharmacist pulled down a shelf of antibiotics and antibacterial tablets. She instructed the girl, who instructed the man, on the dosages and frequencies of the respective pills.

Before the conversation closed, Henri interjected, "Hey, tell her I've got something wrong with my arm."

"What's wrong with your arm?"

"I broke it awhile back and the pain keeps me up at night. Don't let her give you a codeine derivative, tell her I'm allergic to hydrocodone so she…."

She snapped her face around and stared incredulously at Henri, "You're fucked up, no way."

"Try to get a pill called Oxyforte."

"Are you really using me to fish for pain killers? Fuck you, read your dictionary and work that out on your own."

"Fuck you, what's it to you? She doesn't know you. We're already here. Please?"

Her eyes gleamed at the word *please* and she felt a familiar inner tug of mania and codependency. She recalled the sessions she had with Dr. Arcenaux before leaving the States. He warned her it would take years and intense counseling before she would be healed of the abuse her recent love had inflicted upon her. Dr. Arcenaux was convinced the reason she found herself in the same relationship, over and again, was because she mistook intensity for love and was a terrible judge of character. He was adamantly opposed to her traveling until she worked out her inner demons. The girl shrugged off the advice, declared that she needed a change of scenery, and hopped on a plane.

As she mused over what Dr. Arcenaux would think of her current situation, she studied the face of the stranger. He didn't appear to be similar to the men from her past. He seemed softer and weaker and incapable of destroying her. He also needed her to do a favor for him and this made her feel important and more alive than she had felt in weeks. She flashed him an impish smile as she turned toward the pharmacist, "*Yyy, también hay algo con su brazo....*" [And, there's also something with his arm.....]

"I'm Henri Stanton."

"Louise De Mahy."

"Super F"

Eva Mathews

"So French"

Sara Smif

Alternative Architecture

Laura Steadham Smith

These are the blueprints,
he said. He spread them all over the grass for everyone to see. I have

the blueprints. His car fell down the library steps, things spilling from
his trunk: a scythe, rain boots, a djembe. But the important thing

was the blueprints. I couldn't see them from the sidewalk, but I
imagine they had something to do with air

that smells like pine trees or baywater,
blown by wind that gets tangled in the

turbines. Or maybe they were about crab traps and jubilees,
or clouds dappling a buttermilk sky, or old women

with names like June Iris and Della Vaughn. Maybe they outlined
bare feet, and homemade flagpoles hewn with machetes,

and conversations where everyone listens, and trees with
deer in between. Maybe they explained how to go alligator

hunting with a spotlight, a rifle, and a pond. Maybe they showed
how minor chords add color to guitar strings, or how polar opposites

coexist. Or maybe they called that ring around the moon its
glory in the morning. Later, I heard others call the whole thing

an episode: there was a medical explanation for it all. But
was anyone listening?

He had the blueprints

"Strength"

Emily DeLorge

Harriet Tubman In Love

Cynthia Williams

she's hungry
inside
tight calves
cede   she says
words to make
them free
themselves   now
he's always here
there's always
time   unfolding
she breathes
wide cross
his back
and hears
his sigh
Araminta

"From the series *Louisiana Stockyards*"

Beth Kleinpeter

Parish Rd. 319

Sarah Bailly

When you drive South in Louisiana
down one of those little highways
that ends silty, mud-covered, in a boat launch,
you can almost see the coastline receding,
a middle-aged hairline extended East and West as far as you can see.

Spindly live oak trees rise from cheniers
perched in front of elaborate, and not-so-elaborate,
fishing camps built atop pilings and, sometimes, makeshift piers.
Little wooden walkways extend through
tall marsh grass, disappearing into the swamp--
access to an unseen bayou where small,
flat-bottom boats find lunch and dinner,
mostly on weekends.

Catch a glimpse of an old cypress camp,
not soaring into the air, abandoned but
not broken or very much eroded.
Still and silent with Spanish moss dripping from it's porch eaves.
Faint echoes of Zydeco reverberating off the walls
of its two empty rooms.

The crab traps are piled up in the yard
next to the dock. Weeds and wildflowers poke through
the rusting nets, weaving themselves and the traps
into a dense metal and vegetable quilt,
round buoy balls making nice orange and white
polka dots in the pattern of the fabric.

Several shrimp boats are docked with their nets
pulled in tight or completely removed.
The oil or the dispersants or both

have dispersed the shrimpers along the coast,
many signing on to work the rigs--two weeks on,
two weeks off. A lot of time away
from home, too tired to fish when you get back,
but it pays the bills.

It costs a dollar to visit the State Park--
a dollar to see how far back the grass has crept.
A dollar to fill a chest with ice to keep
dinner or lunch fresh as you roll back
up the highway, away from a receding world
toward less-weathered rooms, cotton quilts, and a day job.

"Joan of Arc"

Sara Smif

"Silver"

Elise Toups

Believing in Rice

M. E. Riley

after "Believing in Iron" by Yusef Komunyakaa
(First published in *Eunoia Review*)

The fields survive
every hotdamn summer
but it took decades
to discover how the dollar worked.

They listen to trees filled with locusts
tell you how many are inside
but with the store owners
their math is always off.

Sullied overalls and boots
cross each inch of ground
while thick fingers point.

Their tractor-trailers creak
under another season's load
while sunflowers rise
easy in their lazy autumn domain.

Above beer cans and Dodge's chicken boxes
Riceland smoke erases sunrises
and folks forget rice makes men bend
so close to God's earth.

The hunger under their breath
could anchor down green pines.

Last night, I dreamt seas of green paper
lunch for a child or soldier
out in the fields
running too fast to look 'round.

"Dead Among Living"

Meghan Carter

Miss'ippi

Edna Hawthorne

the smelly old river's pull
confounds one who hails not
from the dirt-clod delta

they could never know of what
they witness before themselves
an endlessly winding brown drain
sucking down noah
and all of animalia

as for the lumber
it got fished out
and that evil pap finn built
a humble drunkard's hovel

you see wood is good
cause wood is dead
and that goes for the nails too

the mighty river feeds on life
so every living thing
on that great big ark
died in that sick river
that stinks of the fever
as it carries deadly parasites
and hundred-year old secrets
of violent flatboatmen
with rotten teeth
downstream
to be hidden
beneath the silt

"Alphabetical Living"

Alicia Hartfield

The House on the Lake

Victoria Moore

Past the second magnolia; across from the lake, of course.
Little Lafourche. We walked those banks, littered with glass shards,
the nail that pushed through my foot, jagged metal roof we slid down.
Everything sharp and glittering; always this wash of light, lack of substance.

It was hot, I know, but I *remember* how the rain smelled of sulfur;
how we'd play in it when the ditches filled to overflowing;
how you stopped to help when I ran through a patch of stickers in the yard.

"Our" tree was hit by lightning—crushed part of the house,
the car. We found a new one, smaller, climbable. (*I dare you*)

You were my brother like that place was mine; the house, Little Lafourche:
all memory, glaring and whitewashed. And without that backdrop,
you're harder to recognize. Foreign, like the far bank.

First Blood at Tiger Truck Stop

Stayja E. Fox

A Prayer for Diana Marston

The graying couple prayed in unison from their bed:

Dear God, please watch over our goddaughter, Diana Marston.
We've tried to keep watch over her, but she escapes it.
We're getting old and slow; we just can't keep up with her.
She thinks that's just because she's lost so much that she's lost everything.
God, please let her know that we love her and that she hasn't lost us.
Give her the strength to forgive those who have wronged her.
Help us to replace her anger with love and happiness.
Amen.

The couple clapped their hands and the lights faded.

CROSSING THE RUBICON

The Felix the Cat wall-clock struck six; Diana awoke to the chorus of her iPhone's *Kill the Eagle Playlist*, which urged her to rise up to the challenge of her rival.

Diana donned a crescent moon necklace with dog tags and applied red war paint below her eyes, which darted between the mirror and a picture of a black Scottish terrier.

Diana slid into the kitchen, where she devoured Frosted Flakes and half of a Cherry Pop Tart, washed down a red pill with Red Bull, and chewed a pink Flintstone's vitamin.

Diana posed in a short green tunic with a longbow in her left hand before a 2010 Acer Netbook and behind a wall dominated by a Geaux Tigers flag, Wonder Woman poster, fan art from Buffy, and Caution: Slow Children Playing sign.

After several web-cam shots, she approached the netbook, chose the picture that emphasized her height and slim hips but downplayed her high forehead, typed a few words, and clicked post.

Diana removed *Conscience of a Conservative* from between *Alice in*

Wonderland and *The Wizard of Oz*, grabbed a semiautomatic Glock-19 with a pink grip, and placed it in the hollow book. She stuffed the book, along with cans of Red Bull and Pop Tarts into a military assault backpack that bore the patch of William M. Marston.

Diana placed her iPhone in an external battery case, listened to the chorus through white ear buds, and refreshed her Facebook page, staring into the blue and white. Her status had received 15 likes within two minutes, a personal best. The die was beyond cast; it had been hurled into the Rubicon. There was no turning back.

HIGHWAY TO THE DANGER ZONE

Revvin' up the engine, listen to her howlin' roar, Diana sang over the roar of the red tractor's engine. In a moment of multitasking magic, she gripped the wheel and typed, "Ridin' Big Red on a highway to the danger zone in a Red Bull rush of nine miles per hour madness past the Neon Bible, the cornfields, and on to The Tiger Truck Stop."

A flashing red and blue siren led Diana to slow the tractor to a stop as the white headphones played Nina Rota and Carlo Savina's *Godfather Waltz*.

A state trooper in his late-forties looked up at Diana, whose crimson-toned impact resistant safety glasses met his dark sunglasses. Diana examined the badge of officer Andi A. Gordon, who had removed his glasses.

"Is there a problem, officer?"

"Get down and take those off."

She complied and stared, unblinking, into the state trooper's hazel eyes.

"Diana, usually I ask for license and registration but considering that…"

Diana, now in the man's shadow, shoved papers into his hands.

"Ms. Marston, I'm no lawyer but it's my understanding that a girl of your age can only drive this tractor on the road for fuel and repairs, but you just passed the gas station closest to your aunt's farm…"

"I'm getting fuel from the Tiger Truck Stop; I want to see Tony."

"Isn't that the one near the Long Land, you know the one with the eagle?"

"I wouldn't know."

"You know Dina likes to follow you on the Facebook."

The state trooper leaned closer; the brim of his hat blocked the sun.

"Well just thirty minutes ago, she texted me something interesting." He read from his cell phone:

The path of all small dogs is beset by the tyranny of the evil eagle Xena. In the name of charity and goodwill, I will strike down upon the eagle that destroyed my precious Toto with great vengeance and furious anger. I am the huntress Diana who will lay vengeance upon thee by turning you into a handbag or hoodie. #vengeanceandfuriousanger

"That was a joke."

"Those arrows a joke too? Seems a joke sharp enough to cut ain't funny."

Diana dodged the state trooper's hazel eyes. "Toto was the first thing that my father gave me after my mother died and before he got shipped out to Iraq, and that eagle just flew off with him like it was…"

"Ms. Marston, turn around."

"The law says I can ride Big Red to the Tiger Truck Stop to refuel."

"I say you can't."

"Fine. I'll just get a ride from someone?"

"Who're you gonna get a ride from?"

"From the line of men who'd do anything to have me in their backseat."

"You don't want to do that, Ms. Marston."

"Just like you don't want to go to anger management."

Officer Gordon's lip quivered. "Ms. Marston, turn around and we'll pretend like this never happened, like the time you maced me."

"You saw me naked."

"You got caught with the Galt boy in his pickup, and I stopped you from making a stupid mistake, just like Bill would have. He's bad news. And how did you thank me, you blinded me for two hours."

"I didn't ask for your help."

"No, you just didn't get pregnant like that Paula Ryan." The state trooper's hat cast a shadow over his face. "Turn around and we'll pretend this never happened."

Diana shut her eyes, focused, and cried to the point of hyperventilation. Officer Gordon stood back, mouth agape.

"I just miss Toto. He's gone forever like everyone else!" Diana's war paint ran like bloody mascara. "I just want...everything keeps falling apart...I just want some control..."

Officer Gordon stepped back and ran his palms over his face.

"When the Westborough Baptist Church protested Bill's funeral. It ate me up. Bill was my best friend and partner, before his unit got called-up. I look at you and I see that little girl who just broke down. One of 'em started yellin' straight at that girl. He looked like a blonde rat that was balding. I'd been biting my lip all day. Now it was just bleedin'."

The state trooper removed his wide-brimmed hat, holding it at his side.

"I was off-duty but I always carry my .45. Always. I crossed the street and pistol-whipped the shit-eating grin off of that face. I was gonna pull the trigger, but I looked at his eyes and couldn't do it. I know what you're plannin' but an eagle is a special kinda creature and I'm pretty certain that when you look at that eagle in its nest with its kin, you're gonna have a mighty weighty moment like mine."

"You should have shot the bastard."

Officer Gordon placed a hand on Diana's shoulder and shed a tear. "I'm so ashamed that I almost did. I got suspended for six months and nearly lost my job."

Diana placed her arms around Officer Gordon. She whispered, "I'm gonna kill that eagle. Anything you do to stop me will just make me want it more."

Officer Gordon shook his head and sighed. "If you promise to look into its eyes, look at its nest, and look at its young'uns, you've got my blessing."

Diana contorted her frown into a half-smile. "Thanks for the blessing."

SMOKE GETS IN YOUR EYES

All who love are blind. When your heart's on fire, you must realize smoke gets in your eyes. Diana sang with her foot on the ignition. Once the tractor passed beyond the state trooper's line of sight, Diana lit a clove cigarette with a chrome United States Army butane lighter, initialized W.M.M. *But today my love has flown away. I am without. I'm without my love.*

As Diana's burning cigarette turned to ash, the *Kill the Eagle Playlist* chorus privately informed Diana through her white headphones that her prison is *walkin through this world alone*, requested that she come to her senses, reminded her that *to resist it is useless, it is useless to resist it*, and asked *where she will stay my little runaway.*

The fiberglass tiger atop the Tiger Truck Stop called out to Diana like the Bat Signal of South Louisiana and the chorus erased any doubts when it released Joan Jett through the white ear buds:

> *Hey street boy, what's your style*
> *Your dead end dreams don't make you smile*
> *I'll give ya something to live for*
> *Have ya, grab ya til you're sore*
>
> *Hello Daddy, hello Mom*
> *I'm your ch ch ch ch ch cherry bomb*
> *Hello world, I'm your wild girl*
> *I'm your ch ch ch ch ch cherry bomb*

Diana walked past the glass door covered with LSU Football and Tea Party decals and made a beeline for the Mountain Dew Code Red and Slim Jims, which she slammed on the purple and gold confederate flag checkout counter.

"John, give me a pack of cloves."

"Do you have I.D.?" A patchy blonde beard with ginger traces surrounded John's smile.

"I forgot it, just like I forgot how we model-T'ed in the back of your Ford, four months back when you knew that Paula was pregnant – speaking of which…is the wedding still two months ago?"

"That brings your total to $23.28."

Diana placed her bow on the counter and stared at his gray eyes through her red impact resistant glasses. The clerk gulped.

"Hypothetically, if a girl is old enough for you to buy her the Morning After Pill then she's old enough for you to buy her cigarettes?"

"That brings your total to $19.13. Also, my Dad wants to see you. He's by the side of the buildin' watching Tony. He's got his shotgun so don't sneak up on him."

Diana smiled. "Thanks, John. Give Paula my best."

As Diana was exiting, John yelled, "And you tell that Godfather of yours that he's lucky I don't sue his ass for that black eye." Diana turned to face John.

"You threaten that man and you threaten me, and you don't threaten a thirteen year old girl who's rockin' a pink gripped Glock-19 inside a hollow copy of *Conscience of a Conservative* and never misses a crotch shot in target practice." Diana would have said more but the white headphones whispered *run, run, run, run, run.*

Diana spied an egg-shaped man, who sat on a rocking chair with a shotgun resting in his lap in front of Tony. Tony, the titular tiger of the Tiger Truck Stop, paced a 10 x 10 foot cell with a red sign that read: No Flash Photography.

"You'd better not be one of those damn hippies threatenin' to steal Tony."

"Mr. Galt, I'd never steal Tony...unless I had the opportunity to feed him to Nick Saban..." Cough-like laughter wobbled the man's jowls. *Pleased to meet you, hope you guess my name,* the chorus whispered through the white headphones.

"You remind me of myself. What with..." The egg-man's words overlapped with the lyrics *but what's puzzling you is the nature of my game.* "...Diana, I'm fat, I'm old, but I'm not stupid – you're goin' onto the Long Land to take what you deserve."

"...actually..."

"Shush yourself, girl, and turn that damn music off. I might be near deaf and those might be off your ears but I can still hear 'em."

Diana muffled the chorus whose last words were *And I lay traps for troubadours who get killed before they reach Bombay.*

"You go and kill that eagle, you're gonna have a hot mess of feds on account of a stupid law that's wrong...that tells a man that he can't care for his own property...damn eco-terrorists claim they're gonna liberate Tony...I think that they meant to kill 'em to make a statement. You tried to stop 'em in the forest but they knocked you out...then they came down here, where I ended their reign of terror..."

"Mr. Galt that story makes no..."

"Every time I think you get close to half the mind of a man, you go and show you got the mouth of a woman!"

"I'm sorry but..."

"It'll make sense because people will want to believe it – facts ain't got nothin' to do with what people say is true!"

"...but..."

"No, buts! Follow the trail covered in hay that way." The egg-man pointed his shotgun to his left. "Scurry along for yer bird watchin.'"

"Mr. Galt how do you know that the eco-terrorists are gonna be takin' that trail or even that they're doin' it today."

"Same way that I know what you're up to."

THE YELLOW TRAIL

Diana followed the hay-covered path and temporary signage that directed visitors to the Long Land and eagle's nest.

"Idiot." Diana muttered.

Within a half mile of her trek, Diana crossed paths with six United Colors of Benetton-looking hipsters in their mid-twenties. Impassioned by M.I.A.'s *Paper Planes*, Diana stopped and folded her arms, blocking their path. "If you cross that path and release that tiger...you're gonna get shot."

The sextuplet of hipsters exchanged glances.

A Zooey Deschanel-looking girl covered her face with vintage aviator goggles and a checkered scarf. The other hipsters followed suit with goggles, bandanas, and the masks of ex-presidents.

The Zooey-looking hipster pointed a black spray can towards Diana. The white ear buds whispered, *lethal poison through their system.*

"What are you..." Before Diana could finish, spicy frothy foam sprayed across Diana's face. "...it burns...is that fucking bear mace..." Diana collapsed onto the yellow trail of hay, coughing.

"Achlach…gragg…" Diana coughed. "…this isn't Brooklyn, you can't just go around macing people…glachhh…"

A man with a rubber Ronald Reagan mask and a faded Exxon shirt turned to the Zooey-looking girl.

"Knock her out, Starbuck."

"You got it, Apollo."

Unable to stop coughing or stand, Diana stared at the black skinny jeans and leggings that dominated her blurry view of the path.

Starbuck bent on her knees and looked into Diana's eyes.

"I am truly sorry for this but you threatened to shoot us…"

"…no…Galt…ACHG…is…gonna…"

Starbuck pressed an unmarked metal container against a fresh rag. "Sweet dreams, Nemo." She pressed the rag against the mouth of Diana, who fell into a deep sleep.

BANG, BANG, BANG

The chorus of the *Kill the Eagle Playlist* continued to whisper to Diana through the white headphones with occasional interruptions from the world:

BANG.

BANG.

Diana awoke next to the trail of hay. The daylight had dimmed. Leaning forward, she vomited Frosted Flakes across the trail. Diana rubbed her eyes until she could see.

.BANG.

She felt for her pack from the forest floor. Grabbing a bottle of Mountain Dew Code Red, Diana poured some over her face and drank the remainder.

::BANG::

::RAWWWRRR::

"AHHHHHHH."

Diana checked her Facebook post for comments and likes. The morning post had reached 115 likes and 37 comments. She had received friend-requests from three of the six eco-hipster-macists.

"Idiots." Diana confirmed the friend requests and walked to the eagle's nest.

The eagle's nest, which was between the size of a large futon and three giant beanbag chairs, sat atop a giant pine tree. Diana determined the best position to deliver a kill shot in a gaze *focused on soaring ambition, consumed in a single desire.*

Diana never noticed the flight of animals or the subsequent silence, only the warning of *The Trees.*

The anticipation-driven adrenaline, the second bottle of Mountain Dew Code Red, and the technotronic pump-up song *Tiger Howl*, which included the synthesized sounds of various tigers, were pumping her heartbeat to warp nine. Diana master of multitasking, saw, heard, and felt everything – but failed to distinguish between the overlapping technotronic tiger beat and the tiger's roar.

I'm just a loner baby, and now you've gotten in my way. Diana sang as she stared at the eagle's nest with a pair of leather-covered binoculars. The setting Sun lit the eagle's release of the top half of a nutria rat into its nest. Diana drew an arrow, raised her long bow, and stared into the eagle as its beak entered its prey, whispering along with the white headphones, *I can't decide whether you should live or die.*

The arrow flew a foot below the nest.

When Diana used her binoculars to reevaluate her position, she saw the eagle feed tiny featherless bobble-headed birds scraps of meat. She remembered her mother pretending that a spoonful of peas were a train and then remembered feeding her mother, bedridden with ovarian cancer on the night before her death.

FIRST BLOOD

Diana noticed that the Facebook post from her Four Square and Facebook check-in at The Tiger Truck Stop had generated a stream of comments such as:

> *Diana, are you okay? Where are you?*
> *Did you release a tiger?*
> *rip Diana*
> *Diana, please call your aunt, she's worried sick.*
> *Get inside of a car or anything with a door....NOW...*

The leaves crackled behind Diana whose neck hair stood on end.

::ROARRRR::

Diana turned to face the tiger whose golden-amber eyes fixated on her. The tiger, whose face was covered with gray foam and left hind leg had been grazed by buckshot, limped closer.

Stepping back, Diana drew the bowstring, aimed, and released a silver arrow into the chest of the charging tiger. When Diana turned to run, the tiger's powerful incisors penetrated Diana's back, causing her to drop the bow. The tiger narrowly missed her spinal column and scattered the contents of her backpack.

The tiger, slowed by the arrow, continued to approach. Since the white ear buds had been pulled from the iPhone, the chorus sang for the tiger, Diana, and all within range of her pocket. Florence and the Machine's *Howl* was replaced with a full marching band thrice interrupted by the cheer, "Go tigers!"

The tiger, now within pouncing range, circled Diana, torturing her with the occasional feint like a housecat to a mouse. The tiger, whose mouth was covered in a mix of Cherry Pop Tarts, pages of *Conscience of a Conservative*, and Diana's blood blocked her path to the bow, arrows, and the backpack's contents.

The pink handle of the Glock 19 contrasted against the shredded, cover photo of Barry Goldwater. Estimating that she could reach the Glock-19 in ten seconds, she raced towards it. The tiger ripped into Diana's left leg in nine.

"Ahhhhh…" Diana rolled to face the tiger's bloody outstretched claws. Diana smelled her blood and Cherry Pop Tarts on the tiger's breath.

::ROARRR::

The tiger's growl pushed Diana deeper into the ground. Diana's camera phone flash temporarily stunned the tiger, allowing her to twist the arrow in the tiger's chest. The phone, which Diana had dropped, automatically loaded the picture as the chorus sang: *1-0-0-1-0-0-1 S.O.S.*

::RAAAAWWKKKK::

The eagle Xena planted her talons in the tiger's back and bit into the tiger's raised paws with her sharp beak. The tiger howled.

Diana pulled herself toward the pink-gripped Glock 19, which she grabbed and pointed at the eagle and Tony, unable to free himself from the eagle's talons.

The panting tiger collapsed onto a bed of red leaves. The eagle, whose knife like talons effortlessly carried away Toto, released the tiger, stared into Diana's eyes, and flew away without any prize. Feeling wet, Diana looked down to discover blood running down her left pants leg.

TIGER EYES

Diana limped toward the tiger until she was certain that she could unload her Glock between the tiger's eyes.

Cataracts fogged the Tony's golden amber eyes, which were sad, angry, and helpless rather than hungry. The chorus tempered Diana's anger:

> *O yonder comes Miss Rosie! How in the world do ya know?*
> *Well, I knowed her by her apron and the dress she wore,*
> *Umbrella on her shoulder, a piece of paper in her han'.*
> *She goes a-walkin' to the captain, said, 'Turn loose my man!'*

Shooting Tony was harder than crushing him with a boulder. Now on her knees, Diana shushed and stroked Tony, singing with the chorus for the tiger. She prayed with her arms wrapped around Tony's once powerful neck until the color of his golden amber eyes changed.

> *Oh, let the Midnight Special shine her light on me,*
> *Let the Midnight Special shine her ever-lovin' light on me.*

After Diana delicately closed Tony's now dull eyes, she sang along with the chorus, until she cried, without trying, for the first time since her father's funeral.

"From the series *Louisiana Stockyards*"

Beth Kleinpeter

Manifesto of the So-Called Gay Agenda

Whitney Mackman

Participant sign at Southern Decadence 2011: "Gay Agenda: 1. Spend time with family 2. Equality 3. Get some milk"

[find a local, national meeting spot]

hold secret secret meetings, so secret
we don't even know about them.
make sure all global gays are in attendance.
must organize pretense for worldwide
brainwashing and cootie-spreading tide
of this especially spectacular disease.

[use adoption for master plan]

since only gay people can produce
a gay child, it would be wild
if we could have families of our own.
we'd create little flaming clones,
teach our kids the tricks of the trade,
grade them on their progress.

[destroy united states army]

due to results of independent research
confirming gayness leads to inabilities
in shooting straight and following orders,
implement Operation Infiltrate:
no barrack, no bunker will be safe from butt
buddies asking and telling all over the place.

[use airports for master plan]

as a matter of national sexuality, all gays
must seek jobs with TSA in current town.

must pat down any attractive, possible
converts and assess the goods they possess.
if they can earn membership, contact
Elton and Ellen for permission to turn.

[make people choose]

because this country is so accepting,
so willing to see gays as human beings
so eager to give us our equal rights,
it is time to make more people choose
to be this way. we must show them
how simple it is to change their DNA.

[appoint leaders for revolution]

it's got to be a macho, macho man,
or a dancing queen, to spin the plan
right round, baby, right round,
and turn back time, to find a way
to wake them up before we go go,
we're coming out - the world should know.

"High and Dry"

Alicia Hartfield

Dad's Boats

Sarah Howze

I watch you with your boats and your wires
mending tiny dials, exhaust risers, gaskets —
all the worlds a clock to you,
something to be adjusted, navigated,
narrated, sailed. You document distance
with constant modulation, calculated
outcomes like tracking currents or tides,
while the Cormorants perch heavy
on the wire over Back Bay. The evening settles in,
which is to be expected in this
scenario, as you adjust and readjust
coils of ropes, cans of gas, various tackle.
You stand swearing below the house, this too
is expected, while you try to get one thing
or another just right for the millionth
time. God bless you and your engineer
heart. Your wife, who is just that because
she has never been my mother,
has trailed off to bed or some other
less interesting waking task. Meanwhile,
I take note of the two baby gators born
last Spring as they emerge from Spartina grass
and circle the dock, amateurs
at low tide navigation. Frogs and cicadas clock
in for the evening hymnal service
as you continue swearing and
adjusting (I don't say fix because I am not sure
if anything was ever broken in the first place).
You are there all night with boat motors, generators,
water pumps and Coast-Guard-issue-radios
trying to learn a language that you don't know
how to speak. You don't know it because it
involves people you love and they don't
process as data. Far as I have ever
been able to tell the fact that you
can't reassemble Dana and me in a manner
you can understand has always
eaten at you just a little bit. The fact that
neither one of us has called in three months
loses its volume in the wake of shrimp
boats coming home with empty nets.

my mother taught me guilt

Anne Delatte

my mother taught me guilt
was a bandage

to be ripped off
every night.

self-adhesive
becomes my skin

a scum of armor to defend
the distended underbelly

of the true and the right—
rewrap me.

now i cannot stick
to a ghost, mother.

this skin has failed
to attract blissful abstraction. i am left

a flapping gash, unglued
raw, steeping

in soul-dirt.

"Amelia"

Molly Gardner

"Blue"

Mercedes Jelinek

SCARS

Cynthia Williams

The children do howl but we grow
to wince, walk the memories back.

Seared lessons in straight lines. Beside
my eye, a chicken pox remnant. Before

a second-grader watched
the *Challenger* spray-dust the 80s,

not casting space as scary as
crack wars, another explosion of film, long before

the confused memory of grandma's flesh-
toned stockings and bandage beneath said

for years, that communion cost
the grafting of one's skin,

lipstick would ruin and eyeliner muzzle
casual eye-wiping, spontaneous tears,

when men couldn't see perfection
in a woman's naked lip after all

the gauze fell down.

Mrs. Vern's Catfish

M. E. Riley

after Frank Stanford

Went down to Mrs. Vern's house
She was cookin supper
Catfish
her and Mr. Joe
had caught somewhere
near the Clarendon bridge
or maybe off Goldman-Sunshine
reservoir where my stepdaddy
takes us so Noah
can ride his four-wheeler
and I can fish.

Gives Mama a break
From what, I'm not sure
Maybe from helpin
me too much.
The worms give my hands
so much trouble
wrigglin like they got a hot date
to get ready for
How could they see
themselves in their lil mirrors
down so far
deep in the dirt?

Mama'll fuss at me
for not doing it myself.
She'll fuss
spit a bit of Skoal in her can
then'll smile
tell me bout the times when
I was real lil
Before puttin em on the hook
I'd kiss the minnows
lips on silver.

No way I'm kissin
worms now
nor minnows for that matter.
I've been wantin to prove
that I can do it
stick the thing
on the hook
then let the bobber
hit the water.

I asked Mrs. Vern
what bait she used
What do the catfish like best?
Must be somethin good
since those fillets she was fryin
were so big
watched two fill
her biggest cast iron.

She chuckled
said she'd tell me
after dinner
She was teachin me
Chinese checkers after
I ate the last hushpuppy.
I asked again
What was it she used
to catch them big catfish?

Mrs. Vern put her green ball down
in my yellow triangle
leaned over the table
til her chair creaked
Chicken livers, she said.
Since Mama rarely bought em
I couldn't help but ask
Did she kiss em?
She howled laughin
said Now baby
what's the point of kissin somethin
that's already dead?

"3 Girls"

Mercedes Jelinek

Sun Tea

Erin Gendron

The jug came from my mother's house. Chipped
at the mouth and scratched inside, I took it with me,
packed in a box with my maiden name scrawled on the side.
As the days get shorter, the steeping takes longer, so I
set it out in the morning, before he leaves for work. The jug
has little diamond impressions, and the sun makes it
shine like a 1000 carats. The prism of it spread across
the deck while the tea bags float like dead goldfish.
I bring it in from the yard and pour in the crystalline sugar, stirring
back and forth at first; then in a figure-8, until the handle
moves on its own, until the tea is dark and clear as beer bottles,
as the autumn night; so cool and sweet sipped from the spoon. Waiting
for dinner, I slice a lemon into little suns. The moths are succumbing
to the porch light when the headlights pass through the house.

I hear footsteps outside, but it's dark, and I can't see
through the screen door. He comes in out of the black,
the sweat on his shirt, like a fingerprint his body made.
The length of his shadow stretches across the table as he grabs the jug,
using two hands to hold it up, the mouth so wide, like a bowl,
like his mouth, but wider. He tips it up and back, and back,
and higher. His throat makes a full sound; deep,
like a heartbeat, and it makes my heart gulp. Tea rushes
over the husks of his lips, spilling down the sides of his mouth,
like he's a vampire in a movie. When the jug is empty, he turns to me,
mouth open and panting; my throat too dry to scream.

"Memories in the Woodwork"

Somer Holloway

Dear Dr. S

Emily Thibodeaux

Dear Dr. S-

So, this is it. The final stretch, the end within sight. In about one year, after I and my fellow editors turn in our proofs to the University of Mississippi Press, we will have the first ever, comprehensive *Dictionary of Louisiana French as Spoken in Cajun, Creole and American Indian Communities*, complete with English to French index. The first thing I learned shortly after I signed on to be a field researcher for this project is that keeping the Cajun culture alive is supremely, an academic pursuit; your average Cajun doesn't care a lick about it. "It's done, it's over with," I was told. "It was a way of life that's no longer viable. We used to be French and now we are American." Yet, in some areas the language persists. Spoken in tight knit groups of elderly Cajuns in greasy spoons and Junior Food Marts before dawn, in nursing homes, between mawmaws and pawpaws, and repeated in the endless renditions of Cajun folksongs that are belted out in dancehalls.

This dictionary, ostensibly, seeks to be more than an academic exercise. We all hope it can be used as a tool to save the language from extinction. For all of us young Cajuns, who know more French than our parents, it is our lifeline to our heritage. That is most of the reason that I became involved. To participate in your romantic quest for the past. You gathered us together, and sent us out into Cajun Country, armed with only tape recorders and legal pads. Most of us knew some Parisian French. It had been taught to us since we were toddlers, in order to try to correct the cultural genocide that began hundreds of years ago when the French Acadians were ousted from Nova Scotia by the British, etc. I can still hear the words spoken by the mythical Evangeline from the video tape you played for us. "Acadie," she whispered mourning her loss. She spoke that word like a longing lover.

The only thing I knew about my own family's history of speaking

French was that my grandparents were whipped with rubber hoses in school if they strayed from speaking English and were made to write 'I will not speak French in school' on the black board. They didn't teach their children, my parents, French. We became a self-contained culture cut off from its source. All our efforts now are for the reparation. Within a single generation, our language was lost. The cost of coming out of isolation has been higher than one might've once thought.

Acadien, ienne [akadʒɛ̃, -dʒɛ̃n, -djɛ̃n] n. Acadian *Et, ça tout amené les Acadians ici.* They brought all the Acadians here. *Chaque hiver les canards et oies refont le voyage des nos ancêtres les Acadians exilés.* Every winter the ducks and the geese redo the voyage of our exiled Acadian ancestors. (ThCa Mille misères) *Là, t'as l'Acadian qu'a arrive. Parce que dans le conte qu'ils ont pour le Grand Dérangement, ils l'ont dispersé de la Nouvelle Écosse, il est venu ici.* Then there is the Acadian who arrived. Because in the tale they have about the exile, they dispersed him from Nova Scotia, he came here.

I didn't want to start at home. I knew that much. It was funny, but I felt like a big fraud, walking amongst all these real people, and here I was with my notebook, observing them, and trying to think of ways to get into a conversation. You'd think I would be a people person, but I'm really not. I can think of a million question beforehand, but when I am actually asking those questions, I feel like I have no business talking to strangers, and that I would be understanding, even relieved, if they were to decline. Anyway, I thought that I could pluck up some courage by starting out in a cemetery. I went to Lyon's Point, into the woods, where nobody lives, and sat down on a broken tomb near a cypress. I wasted a whole day there, feeling sorry for myself. I'm sorry. I didn't think that I would be this forthcoming, but I can't help, but be honest with you. Chastise me.

Shayne Barr, author of *The Cajuns: The Americanization of a People*, says that in Louisiana, the Cajuns, on the bayous and prairies in the deep south, existed, barely aware of the Civil War. They called it "La Guerre des Confederats." Those Cajuns who were drafted, deserted. A whole regiment of Cajun deserters were shot and killed, and were buried on the spot, in the Lyon's Point cemetery. I think I have relatives buried out there too. It was a bittersweet feeling that the place gave to me, a feeling of gravity.

It's almost humorous to think of the Cajuns, ignorant of people like Abraham Lincoln, and later, probably even Hitler, farming, pumping their German accordions with their thick red hands, yodeling out-of-tune sob stories, waltzing in their dancehalls, singing ballads addressed to the interminable Jolie Blonde, and foot stomping to two steps at great fêtes near the waters of Bayou Pompon. To tell you the truth, my mother hated those songs. When she grew big enough, she moved to a bigger city and tried to forget them.

I wish that I could ever remember to take detailed notes while in the field. It would save so much time, not having any transcribing to do. But I can't ever find the time to write while trying to make conversation with the goal of extracting information. This is why I brought the tape recorder in the first place, you remember I was averse, but I can't quite think of it as a friend, even now.

I usually spend an hour driving, depending on where I'm going, just talking to myself until I forget the recorder's there. It's a bit hard. I don't know if I can ever feel entirely comfortable. It would be like loving an insect, all hard carapace and sensors. I have consistently never been able to love any creature without hair. Like pets I mean. I feel the exact inverse about humans. Anyway, I am already off topic. You know how I can get.

I was on Highway 92 passing through the tiny city of Maurice. It's a suburb of Lafayette, the Hub City, supposedly, but where Cajuns and non-Cajuns alike go to open business or to attend the University of Louisiana at Lafayette. Most everybody who lives in the suburbs like this work off-shore in the oil field. 92 passes through Milton, which seems to me to consist of a trailer park and a Catholic Church with the largest parking lot that I have ever seen. There's a small bridge that you pass before you are truly on your way to Vermillion Parish, 95% of the people who live in Vermilion are Cajun, and I've been doing all my interviews there. There's an unmistakable bridge over the Vermilion River. On one side of the road there is a used car lot, with rusted truck bed roofs and tires stacked in futuristic mazes. On the other side is a small bar. It is downhill from the road and as I pass over the bridge my eye always stops there. It's a corrugated metal structure with a hand painted sign. The best part is that someone took the time to paint a large yellow smiley face on the side of the building. Its eyes are too close together to be a stencil, but it does the job.

One day, I stopped off in the bar. It was a truly shitty place. There were only three bar stools, none of which matched. All they served were bottles of Bud light and cans of Pabst. There was no place to store anything else, so close to the water, and kegs were not safe from mildew, so nothing was on tap. I was full of a mounting enthusiasm to capture the local vibe. I didn't quite know that a different breed of Louisianians were to be found drinking in that little dank hole on a Tuesday afternoon. The whole place was a skinny rectangle, two largish people couldn't fit side by side with their arms stretched out. I was in the C's then, and still feeling optimistic. There were two patrons there, sucking down buds and filling the room with stale smoke. I came up to the bar and ordered a beer in my best French. *"Une bière, s'il vous plaît."* The men looked down from the small brown t.v. where they were watching a baseball game.

"What?" the bartender said.

"Oh, I'm sorry. I thought that maybe you were Cajun." He was older, with a large beer gut and a baseball cap on his head. He had the black eyes and the prominent nose.

"No," he said, cracking open a new beer and slopping some down his front as he drank. "I'm not a coonass. There ain't any coonasses in here today."

So here I bring you:

COONASS [kunas] n.m. [pej.] coonass, insulting nickname for a Cajun (used by Anglophones).

Good times. I took the beer and made my way out, whispering the definition into my trusty tape recorder. I sat in my hot car, baking in the sun, and sucked down the beer until a fierce belch ripped at my nose. I baked myself until light headed to try to ease my embarrassment.

Just before the turn off to Kaplan, 'the most Cajun place on earth,' is a restaurant called Soup's. They will cook just about anything that walks on four legs, or at least that's what my latest contact Pop Pop Duhon told me. He is an octogenarian Cajun fiddler, who is tall and skinny, has a nose like a chicken hawk, and always sports a uniform of a one piece khaki jumpsuit, mesh backed John Deere hat, and two strap Velcro sneakers. He also has a penchant for alligator meat, and has been known to shoot and eat Nutria rats, the outsize rodents that were introduced to the bayou from Asia. They have no natural predators, sport long orange teeth, and copulate like rabbits.

nutria [njutria, nutra] n.m./f. nutria, coypu
"Deep fried and with some Tony's Chacherie's, *cher. Ca c'est bon!*"
Most of my words are from him. His other entry is: "Aye ye yaille!" (Spelling is variable.)

ayayaie (aïe, aïe-aïe) [ajajaj] interj. oh, ouch *Ayayaie! Tu me fais mal.*
Ouch! you are hurting me.

When I met him, I accidentally stepped on his foot. He was teaching me to two-step at Randall's, an overpriced Cajun dance-hall and restaurant. Every Saturday morning the Acadiana Open channel broadcasts couples dancing to a live Cajun band. It's the most dull thing that I've ever seen on T.V. The camera is stationary for most of the time, giving a long shoot of the band on stage, chan-ky-chanking (new word?) and geriatrics stiffly whirling around each other. It was pretty fun to do in person, jigging with the old man I just met. He called me cher (pronounced sha) and reminded me of my grandfather. When the music changed into a slow waltz, Pop Pop, who was surprisingly spry for a man of eighty, hopped up on stage, grabbed an accordion from a stunned musician and began to sing. It was the WWII classic, J'ai Passé Devant Ta Porte. Here it is transcribed for your pleasure. Imagine it being tonelessly crooned by an over the hill Cajun man stooped over in a chair with an enormous Hohner accordion on his knee. This is how they sing it.

J'ai passé devant ta poooooorte.
J'ai crié bye-bye la belle,
N'a personne, qui m'a reponduuuuu.
Aye yé yaille, mon coeur fait mal!

And my, inexpert translation, hopefully I didn't major in French for nothing:

I passed in front of your door.
I yelled, bye-bye my lovely.
No one answered back.
Oh Shit! My heart, it hurts.

When he sang the soaring refrain '*Aye yé yaille!*', he pointed down to his toes, and then back at me and cackled. It's a sad song. I know it might seem funny to you, but you should hear how these old men sing these songs! It makes you ache right from the bottom. Remember how you said you sometimes drink when you're alone? I've been doing it too, but nobody does that here. Since that day at the riverside bar, I've been stocking up at night. Goodnight, you. (I hope you're not rolling your eyes behind your rimless frames).

I have so many sound clips from Pop Pop! All recorded and stored on miniature tapes. The way I've been working is that I listen to the last entry that I recorded to get back in the swing of things. It also helps me with the alphabetization. I've been operating in a heat and beer haze, so my entries have been a little haphazard. (Are you going to fire me? =))

Anyway, after dancing, Pop and I met a few more times. Once, I visited him in his garage where he kept a wood burning stove and an old plaid couch. The first thing he says on that tape is, "They was gunna cut off my foot, cher. *Cher mondieu! Un pied perdu!*" He had diabetes and blue bruises climb up his legs. All the old people are getting it. I had asked him why. He told me:"It's the food. It's the change in lifestyle. Yeah, we ate bad. We butchered the pigs and kept the lard in glass jars to cook with, but we worked it off. We all worked hard. I used to farm, rice and soy beans, but now my land is subsidized. I get a check from the government every month to let the land lay fallow. It's barely enough to get by. Now I don't know what it is they feeding us. (I think he receives food from the government, or from some sort of charitable organization). We never did complain very much. We always did what they said, but I always thought they was trying to kill us."

Perdre [paed(r)] Iv.t.r. I to lose *On a tout perdu.* We lost everything.

Could you imagine what it would feel like to lose everything? I've been wondering if you've ever really missed someone. Are you the type of person who doesn't really need anyone else? I remember you once told me you could live in a cave and be a real hermit. Like it's some sort of genetic predisposition. I didn't believe you at the time. But now I really would like to ask you. I probably won't keep this in, but right now, it's 10:30 on a Friday, and I'm lying on top of the comforter at the Holiday Inn, drunk, with all my clothes on, and I'm wondering if you miss me.

It's been kind of hard to keep my cheer up. LA 696 is surrounded by fields, as far as the eye can see. This is flat land. Nothing pulls the gaze upward, and I notice that I've been feeling stuck. Walls of burning sugar cane rise on either side of my car as I plunge into Vermillion Parish. Burning bits of cane drift down from the sky. I always wonder how it could get so high up their before falling down again.

So far, I've canvassed almost all of Vermilion parish, searching for all 100 of my words. Finding local bilingual people to use their quotations as explanations for the word's usage. I know that there are too many people to count. But I really feel averse, at this point, to keeping their submissions anonymous. Their words tell a story of their lives. Pop Pop's life is in fragments in my tiny tapes.

However, before I rebuke you too strongly for what I consider to be a strange decision, I have some confessions to make. I never spoke in French to Pop Pop Duhon and he never spoke in French to me. I had tried at first, but my accent was so strange to his ears. My diction, like Count Dracula, was learned out of a text book. At the dancehall, he would turn to middle aged Cajuns sitting at the bar and query "*Quoi ça dit, cher?*" "What did she say?" They knew even less French than I did, though their voices in English struck the same cadences as a native speaker. I thought of my great grandmother in the nursing home in Crowley, with two whole generations of her offspring cut off from her in the most vital way. How could she pass on her stories? How could I possibly know about her life? She spoke no English at all. Most young Cajuns, I've met think that they don't need the language to maintain their culture. People my parents age, who unlike my mother, stayed and carried in the beat down town, living in their nice houses next door to derelict shacks. Working as educators, in their trades at the hospital, and on oil rigs in the Gulf. No longer self-sufficient, but schizoid, and deluded. I thought that maybe I could change it. I signed up for this project, even with its meager salary. While we were working, the budget for education got cut in half, and then half again. I know that you know this, and that we worked through it, but I have to say after all my studying, I came up empty. As much as I might look Cajun and have my pretty French last name, I am, for all intensive purposes, a foreigner. As much as we tried, deep in my gut, I know this project is a failure.

Did you know that no one in the town will talk to me anymore? That Cajuns are the most suspicious of any people that I've met? Do you know who turned me away first? My own family. I came around to interview them, my aunt and my grandfather.

"I don't need to know the language to be Cajun," my aunt told me. "Cajun is about family. It's about the food, the family gatherings and a willingness to help each other out." She had no French words for me, and became agitated when I tried to stress the important of speaking the language. "We are French, we are Catholic. We eat Cajun food and play Cajun songs. What else is there?" And I couldn't argue with her. Since leaving home, I had become a vegetarian. I didn't eat Cajun food. I didn't play Cajun songs. I was not Catholic and did not receive the Eucharist at mass. Since the age of ten, when my aunt and grandmother died of cancer, I no longer believed in God. I was antithetical to all traditions. Like my great grandmother, the real Cajuns did not recognize me. They might have opened their arms to embrace me, but we sat mute, staring kindly into each other's eyes, before excusing ourselves.

It was my grandfather who gave me those words: "It's done, it's over with. It was a way of life that's no longer viable. We used to be

French and now we are American." He refused to speak in French with me after that. In fact, he barely speaks to me at all. At family gatherings he shows up, overweight, tired looking, hungover, eats his fill of rice and gravy and falls asleep in the recliner.

Pop Pop Duhon only talked to me because he was stricken with grief. He told me this story on tape five. His wife had always been barren, and in her later years opted for a hysterectomy. They had driven in his old tan Toyota pick-up truck to the Abbeville General Hospital for the procedure. They had done a biopsy, opened her up, and found that her ovaries and uterus were full of cancer. It was so advanced that all they could do was close her up again. She died a month later, and was buried at the sunken graveyard in Lyon's Point, along with the ancient Confederate dead. I had asked him that if he could go back, would he even want to live like they used to. Illiterate farmers, living in the sticks and on the edge of bayou with no running water or electricity, working hard with their families, telling the old stories and playing the old songs. He offered me this gem:

misérable [miserable(l)] adj. miserable, unfortunate, pitiful, destitute. *J'aimerais que ça pourrait revenir comme c'était dans les vieux temps, mais on serait bien misérables parce que tu pourrais pas faire les enfants travailler.* I wish things could go back to the way they were in the old days, but we'd be miserable because you'd never get the kids to work.

He chuckled a little after he told me that one, and put his hand on my shoulder. He looked at me solemnly in the eyes and then said in English, "Just what is it that you really want from me?" he asked.

I didn't see him after that. I had my quota. I had done my job. I went back to the University Place Apartments and compiled the information in the text file that I will attach.

Two weeks later, I found myself, once again, turning onto Highway 14, taking a right towards Cushing Street, Kaplan's tiny main street. There is a bank, two closed down gift shops and a roller skating rink. That's all there is, besides a small historical museum on my left, "La Musée de la Ville de Kaplan." It is full of yellowed archives of the *Kaplan Herald*, and is run by yet another well meaning person who can't understand my French. I've only been in once. It seems that my embarrassment is fathomless.

After turning off of Main Street, and taking a right onto American Legion, there's a large Sonic Drive-in on my left. It put out of business an old burger and shake place, Mickey's, which used to be on the other side of the road, facing it. My mom told me she used to eat there, and that they had the best crushed ice. The dusty blue awning is still there, hanging where you used to be able to drive in for burger and curly fries. There is a ghost of the white lettering still visible. A washed out "M."

The last building on the road is like no other structure in Vermilion Parish. It is a large brown building, shaped like a pointed roof. The sides come down nearly to the pavement and the front peak creates an awning through which car can pass. Or more importantly, a hearse. The funeral home has only one parlour, so at least, for once I would avoid becoming confused. Someone had thought that I was a relation, and told me the news when I had asked about him at the restaurant the day before. He had fallen into a diabetic coma a week after our last meeting, and died the night before, at Abbeville General, while sleeping.

I'm not saying that I thought you should've flown down for the funeral. I had reservations myself. I didn't know anyone there. I most definitely did not know all of the complicated hand motions and responses to call back to the priest at the Holy Rosary Cathedral during the funeral mass. But I went anyway. I guess what I really want to say is that if you are not putting his name into the credits for the dictionary, I want my name taken out as well. If he is to be disappeared into obscurity, so am I.

Now that I am made bold by grief, I'll just say what it is that I wanted to say. I know we both promised we wouldn't talk about it, and I know you have a wife. I've met her. I mean, is she a bitch? She seems maybe a little too skinny, and her smile is stretched too thin. Do you ever think sometimes that maybe you might make her feel bad about herself, and she is spite-starving herself? Doesn't she spend all that time at the gym because you're always up at school?

I'm sorry. I know I don't know anything about your relationship with Tanya. I just always got the impression, when I was up in your office, that you lived in there. I mean, you have a couch, and hundreds of boxes of thin mints. I mean, do you have a daughter who is a girl scout, or do you just buy them en masse and freeze them? It's a little insane, right, to wonder about those things. I have to tell myself that we only kissed once. And it was right after we got that grant money, and we both hadn't slept for five days, and maybe it couldn't have been an accident, or the tequila, just skin brushing, you know? But you reached, you *reached* forward, and pulled my head to yours. I can't forget how that felt, to be rushed forward, not really knowing where I would end up. That moment lasted forever. That reach, that pull.

I don't think I can come back to school.

I won't retract my research, but please leave my name out of the finished text. That is all. I've got to get out of here. I'm not sure where. All that I know is that as I watched Pop Pop's coffin descend into the earth, I felt a sinking in my core. An old and bitter sadness that was larger than me got its fingers into me, and it will consume me if I stay. I think this land has ghosts. I think now I'll have to search for a place where I belong, or else I will die. I know you'll say to come back, but as you know, it can never be the same as before. You haven't spoken to me in a month, and I don't think I can do this. I might only ask you one thing if I see ever you. You might have come across it in your research as Chair of Cajun and Creole Languages at the University of Maine. I've asked so many Cajuns, but no one could tell me the answer.

What's the Cajun word for home?

Sincerely,
Me

"L'église"

Amanda Harb

Contributing Belles

Sarah Bailly left New Orleans city life in 2011 to start a farm in South Louisiana. Currently, she spends her days tending to her flocks of sheep and chickens and watching the grass grow.

Jade Benoit grew up in South Louisiana and received a B.A. in English from Louisiana State University. She is currently finishing her MFA in Poetry from the University of North Carolina - Wilmington. Her work has appeared and is forthcoming in *Black Warrior Review*, *Nashville Review*, *LUNGFULL! Magazine*, *Smoking Glue Gun Magazine*, and *Apalachee Review*.

Emily Bufford was born and raised in New Orleans and is proud to still call the Crescent City her home. Along with writing, she particularly enjoys teaching freshman composition and wearing alternative hair extensions.

Meghan Carter is a law student by day and a law student by night. In between reading rules and regulations, cases and commentary, she finds herself reading literature, looking at art, and listening to music. And so she is both humbled and proud to become a published Belle.

Anne Delatte holds a B.A. in English/Creative Writing from Louisiana State University. She is currently at large working on language projects around the Baton Rouge and New Orleans area.

If making art as an active artist is like the exhaust from a running vehicle, the question is... What's your fuel? - **Emily DeLorge**, Thibodaux, Louisiana

Jenilee Domingue is a portrait and landscape photographer in Prarieville, Louisiana. She loves to snap photos when she travels to different locations. http://jenilee-d-photography.com.

Stayja E. Fox is clearly a penname based on a fever-induced dream that took place during an Indian brownout. Stayja enjoys reading almost everything but prefers to write material that explores human identity and relationships. The E stands for Evangeline.

Georgia Frederick is Fire, Ice, and Passion.

Molly Gardner is a photographer based out of Chattanooga, Tennessee. Her photography illustrates the simple beauty of daily life through a photojournalistic perspective. "Photography holds the ability to capture the subtle nuances of a situation, giving my viewers access to all the depth and beauty that a single moment in time can possess." www.facebook.com/MollyGardnerPhotography

Erin Gendron is originally from Michigan but has resided in the south for the past 7 years and considers it to be her adopted home. She received an MFA from the University of New Orleans and now lives in the Atlanta area.

Erin Paige Grauel has her MFA from the University of New Orleans. Though she hails from the oceans of South Carolina she currently lives in a puddle in New Orleans. She would not have it any other way.

Amanda Lilah Harb hails from the Cajun country of Lafayette, Louisiana. She is currently finishing law school at the University of Amsterdam focused in environmental law. But in all her wanderings, she brings with her the vibrant spirit of the south.

Alicia Hortman Hartfield is a natural-light photographer and a mother of four. www.aliciahartfieldcreative.com.

A Louisiana native, **Edna Hawthorne**, is a 29 year old freelance country lady, and a proud Southerner. Much to the chagrin of federal, state and local officials, she, along with her two sons and a handful of close associates, currently operates a self-sustaining free-range chicken and poppy farm, deep within the Kisatchie National Forest.

Janey Hogan was raised in a family of educated Southern Democrats. She roamed through her childhood writing plays, turning cartwheels, and laughing with her beautiful sisters. This is why she is as she is.

Liz Hogan lives in Hammond, Louisiana and is currently pursuing an MFA degree in Poetry at the University of New Orleans. She enjoys rocking out and writing songs with her wife Lilli in their band The Shiz and is the proud sister of Belle Journal founder, Janey. www.shizrock.com

At 23 years old, photography has been **Somer Holloway**'s passion since she can remember. Somer surrounds herself with art, beauty and uniqueness and strives to capture the world in the truly magnificent way she sees it.

Sarah Howze is a Mississippi Gulf Coast native, who flew the coop at seventeen to attend college and live on both coasts due to her partiality to temperate climates, palm trees, and beach bums. She returned home after Hurricane Katrina on a crisis sabbatical. One year later, she found herself in New Orleans and fell madly in love with the city. She is now finishing her M.A. at the University of New Orleans in English, with a concentration in American Literature and Modern/Contemporary poetry.

Mercedes Jelinek received a B.F.A. from the State University of New York at Purchase and an M.F.A. from Louisiana State University. She currently is continuing the second part of her "Photo Booth Project" in Brooklyn, New York. http://www.mercedesjelinekphotography.com.

Kelly Jones tried to come up with a clever bio, but did not succeed. She's from NC, lives in New Orleans, and will soon have an MFA in poetry from UNO's Creative Writing Workshop. When not writing and reading poetry she can be found teaching, dancing, doing improv, or barista-ing with the best of 'em.

Beth Kleinpeter grew up on a farm in southern Louisiana, and graduated with a bachelor's degree in Photography from Louisiana State University. She currently resides in Baton Rouge, where she is working as a freelance photographer.

Whitney Mackman teaches Freshman Composition and is about to finish her MFA in Poetry at the University of New Orleans. When she is not corrupting the future minds of America, she can be found exploring New Orleans, reffing lacrosse, and drinking her weight in chocolate milk.

Andi Malisheski's hometown is Katy, TX, although she loves her adopted city of New Orleans, where she is pursuing an undergraduate degree in Creative Writing at Loyola University. Andi has a fiction novel in the works and one day she hopes to work in publishing to help other writers, like herself, share their hard work and passion with others.

Eva Mathews is a psychiatrist finishing her training in Boston. Just as soon as she's done, she (and her southern gentlemen husband and baby son) are going to run back to the south!

Carly Melancon came to Austin via Baton Rouge in 2007, after graduating from LSU. She is in the Nursing program at ACC and consumes massive amounts of media in her spare time.

Victoria Moore is a southern poet, whose work has a strong sense of place. She currently teaches at LSU after receiving an MFA from West Virginia University. She has poems published in *Zone 3 Magazine* and *The Albion Review*.

Lynda Lou Plunkett is 5'3" of bones, blood, dirt and glitter. An adventure lover, mother-wife and free woman with no place free to roam.

Persephone Pontelier comes from a town on the banks of Bayou Lafourche, where she grew up believing that all the ground in the world is wet when you dig three inches down into it. She has never seen a basement.

M.E. Riley currently tramps through Louisiana swamps; the cigarettes burn, the whiskies sweat, and she'll tell her stories to anyone who stops by for a spell. She is an Assistant Poetry Editor for *Bayou* literary magazine, as well as a regular contributor to *Bayou*'s blog. Work is forthcoming or has appeared in *Euonia Review*, *Occupy Poetry*, and *Tales from the South VI*, among others.

Laura Steadham Smith's work has appeared in *Mental Floss* and the *Florida English Journal* and has been read on Florida's NPR affiliate. When she's not teaching freshman composition, she enjoys misreading recipes and learning the mandolin.

Gladys Cagle Tritico Stoker was a Belle in the truest sense of the word. She was born in Merryville, Louisiana in 1922 and was considered different even then because she would walk in the rain and sing. She married Frank Tritico, her former high school history teacher, in 1939. She had six children and lived in Lake Charles. She searched for the Fountain of Youth for several years and backpacked Australia and New Zealand at the age of 73. She died in 1998.

Stephanie Kadel Taras, Ph.D., grew up in West Virginia, went to college in Florida, and now resides in Ann Arbor, Michigan, where she writes life stories and institutional histories through her company, TimePieces Personal Biographies. Her unpublished nonfiction book, *Mountain Girls*, about the lives of West Virginia women, won a West Virginia Writers book prize in 2012.

Emily Thibodeaux is from Lafayette, Louisiana. She graduated from Columbia University in 2012 with an MFA in Fiction. Emily currently lives in Lafayette and teaches English at South Louisiana Community College. She is at work on her first novel and also a play.

Elise Toups is a Louisiana native. She has a background in Psychology and Painting from Louisiana State University and is currently working toward her MFA at Michigan State University. www.elisetoups.com.

Lori Wainwright was born and raised in southern Louisiana and in turn, raised her three beautiful daughters there as well. As early as age ten, Lori was writing and telling stories to her younger siblings. Through light-hearted, rhyming stories Lori finds that she is often able to rejuvenate her spirit and recapture, however briefly, the carefree, mindset of her youth. The poem, "Jacques De Grille" was an interactive poem Lori composed with her daughter, Danielle Armbruster, when she was four.

A native New Orleanian, **Cynthia Williams** lives in Atlanta, Georgia. Her nonfiction has been featured in *New Orleans CityBusiness* and *Frugivore* online magazine.

18472203R00073

Made in the USA
Charleston, SC
05 April 2013